How to Make a
Too Cool
T-shirt Quilt

Andrea T. Funk

Smilie Press

How to Make a Too Cool T-shirt Quilt

Smilie Press
5225 S Stine Rd
Olivet MI 49076
269-749-9249

Find us on the Web at www.toocooltshirtquilts.com

Editor: Roger L. Funk
Cover Design: Roger L. Funk
Cover Photographs: Roger L. Funk
Internal Photographs: Milie T. Funk, Roger L. Funk and Andrea T. Funk
Proof Reader: Sarah Bendure

ISBN **0-9771169-0-5**

Printed and bound by Color House Graphics, Inc, Grand Rapids Michigan

Dedicated To

David R. Johnson
Thank you for believing in me and my
crazy dreams.

Milie T. Funk
You are the best daughter anyone could
ever hope to have.

Table of Contents

Foreword

Since first publishing this book 4 years ago, I have made over 900 T-shirt quilts. During this time, I hired employees to help me and taught classes about making Too Cool T-shirt Quilts. It was through this teaching that I discovered that I knew more about making T-shirt quilts than I realized. As a result, I have added many hints, tricks and techniques to this book to make it even easier for you to make a Too Cool T-shirt Quilt.

I hope you enjoy making your Too Cool T-shirt quilt.

Andrea T. Funk

2009

Chapter 1

Introduction

A T-shirt quilt is a soft and durable way to preserve the memories of your T-shirts. When someone sees their new T-shirt quilt for the first time, their memories come flooding back. They point to a block on the quilt and start telling you about it: "I got this T-shirt at a Race for the Cure 5K. It was my first race…." And then they point to the next T-shirt and you see the memories in their eyes.

Mickey Mouse T-shirt Quilt

A T-shirt quilt lets you wear all your T-shirts at once… it's like having your cake and eating it too! Many people are so attached to their T-shirts that they can't let them go. But once they see what can become of their T-shirts, parting with them becomes a little easier. In the years that I have been making T-shirt quilts, I have cut some very special T-shirts. The owners of these T-shirts are always happy when they see their new quilt with all their special T-shirts. The quilt becomes a treasure while at the same time easing the stress on an over-stuffed dresser.

Too Many T-shirts

So, you have been asked by someone with too many T-shirts to make a T-shirt quilt. Your first question is: how? This book will walk you through each step of making a Too Cool T-shirt Quilt.

I began making T-shirt quilts in 1992 when my sister Karen arrived at my door with a large plastic bag full of T-shirts. Karen, a triathlete, had too many T-shirts. Every time she raced, she picked up another T-shirt. She told me that she had heard about other people making quilts out of their T-shirts and asked me to make one. At that time, I was making traditional quilts and I had no idea how to make a T-shirt quilt. I asked her, "How?" She said that she didn't care. Hardly helpful directions!

I spent some time studying her T-shirts. I looked at how the T-shirts were printed, the size of the printing, and the placement of the printing. I experimented with cutting and sewing T-shirt material. And, I spent a lot of time pondering the challenge. Then I had the "Ah-ha moment" and, as they say, "the rest is history."

When I was studying the T-shirts, I noticed that some had large designs (left photo) while others had very small designs (right photo). I needed a way to integrate all the different sized logos into a quilt. To accommodate the different sizes, I based my design for the quilt on a 4" square. By using blocks that are divisible by 4, I can cut my block to fit each individual design

Large Design 12" x 12"   Small Design 4" x 4"

on the T-shirt. For example, a T-shirt with a small design on the front might call for a 4" square block, while the design on the back might need to be cut with a block that was 12" x 12". As long as each block used is divisible by 4, that block can be used in the quilt. The result is a quilt top with many sized blocks. It is a break from the traditional T-shirt quilt with sashing.

When I started making T-shirt quilts I did not know that *"You are supposed to back each of the T-shirts with some type of stiff backing and sew them together with cotton sashing."* Since I didn't know this, I just sewed the T-shirts to one another without any backing. It worked! As a result, a Too Cool T-shirt Quilt is soft and flexible, unlike a traditional T-shirt quilt with backing and sashing.

It is the combination of a design built around blocks divisible by 4 and sewing the blocks to one another without backing or sashing that makes a Too Cool T-shirt Quilt unique. This design principle also enables you to use a large number of T-shirts in one quilt. This is a real plus for runners or swimmers with 60 or 70 T-shirts.

Andrew's Swimming T-shirt Quilt

There are endless varieties of T-shirt quilts that can be made with this method and they cannot all be listed here, but here are some ideas:

- Sports Quilts – made from T-shirts from one team, one sport or the athletic events one has done. (Right)

Edie's T-shirt Quilt

- Baby or Kid Quilt – made from baby or kid T-shirts or made out of found baby and kid T-shirts. (Left)

Baby Sarah's T-shirt Quilt

- College or University Quilts – made from one school or a variety of schools. (Left)

Michigan State University T-shirt Quilt

- Corporate Quilt – made from T-shirts gathered from co-workers. A corporate quilt makes a great gift for Founders, CEOs or other executives or retirees. (Below)

Incredible Technologies T-shirt Quilt

- Family Quilt – made from T-shirts from all family members, from family functions or from family vacations.

- Anniversary Quilt – made from T-shirts that celebrate any type of anniversary.

- High School/College Graduation Quilt – made from the graduating student's T-shirts. This is a very popular type of T-shirt quilt. The quilt is displayed at the open house and everyone talks about the events on the T-shirts. This is a true memory quilt.

Breanna's High School Graduation T-shirt Quilt

Close-Up of "Taz" Theme T-shirt Quilt

- Theme Quilts – made from T-shirts that reflect the theme of your choice. Some ideas are:
  o Animals
  o Vacations
  o Cartoon Characters
  o Number quilt

- Memorial Quilts – made from T-shirts and clothing of a deceased loved one. Instead of throwing away the T-shirts and clothing of a loved one, a block or two of material is used from each clothing item to make a very special quilt. I know from experience that these quilts are a valuable way to help cope with a loss. They will make you cry, but they will also bring you joy.

Getting Started

If you have prior quilting experience, you will need to disregard some, but not all, traditional quilting rules. If you don't have any quilting or sewing experience, you should do well if you follow these directions closely and practice the skills before cutting up your favorite T-shirts. Wherever your skill level falls, however, I would suggest that you make your first quilt a small one. You might even think about going to second-hand stores or garage sales and buying 10 to 15 T-shirts to make a trial quilt.

Before you begin your quilt, I suggest that you read through all the steps presented in this book. Why? First, you need to know what tools and materials you will need. For example, you will need to go to a hardware store to purchase acrylic plastic (Plexiglas®) for the templates. Second, you need to understand what will happen at each step. This will insure that there are no surprises. It will also help you plan ahead and move from step to step with ease.

Tweety Bird T-shirt Quilt

Coca-Cola & Dalmatian Dog T-shirt Quilt

Chapter 2
Gathering the T-shirts

The first step in making a T-shirt quilt is gathering the T-shirts. This is a critical planning stage in making a quilt. The T-shirts you put into the quilt will *always* be in the quilt. When I first began making T-shirt quilts, I made a small quilt for Jennifer which included the back of a T-shirt that had an advertisement on it. To this day, every time I see Jennifer, she asks me if I can take this T-shirt out and replace it with another one. And, sadly, I can't.

> Remember: The T-shirts you put into your quilt will always be there. If you don't like the T-shirt now, you most likely will not like it in the future.
> **Choose carefully!**

The next big question is: "How many T-shirts are needed?". This is a difficult question to answer. It depends upon what size quilt you want. If you want a large quilt, more T-shirts are needed. If you want a small quilt, fewer T-shirts are needed. It also depends upon what size the designs are. If the designs are large, then fewer T-shirts will be needed. But if the designs are small, more T-shirts will be needed. If there are designs on the front and back of the T-shirt, then fewer T-shirts will be needed. But if there is only a design on one side of the

T-shirt, more will be needed. It also depends upon how many T-shirts you have. Below is a chart of approximately how many T-shirts you *may* need.

	Size	# of T-shirts
Lap	48" x 48"	15–20
Large Lap	52 x 68"	20–30
Twin	60" x 84"	30–40
Full	84" x 92"	40–50
Queen	92" x 100"	50–60
King	100" x 112"	60–80

Generally, I start with the number of T-shirts I have, cut them and then see what size quilt they will make. It is after the cutting stage that you can determine how large your quilt will be. This is one departure from traditional quilting where you decide on the size quilt before you begin.

Where to Get T-shirts or More T-shirts

Often, people decide to make a T-shirt quilt because they have a dresser drawer overflowing with T-shirts. I have made quilts for men who say, "My wife says it's me or my T-shirts." A T-shirt quilt is a perfect solution to this problem. But after you have emptied the dresser and all the boxes and you still don't have enough T-shirts, where can you go for more T-shirts?

Here are some places that I have gone to find more T-shirts:

- Family
- Friends
- Co-workers
- Classmates
- Garage Sales
- Second hand shops – e.g. Goodwill
- Lost and founds

Things to Consider

One consideration has to do with the colors of T-shirts as they relate to the final quilt. A mix of colored and white T-shirts works best because it provides a balance between the light value of the white T-shirts and the darker value of the colored T-shirts. I have made a number of quilts using only white T-shirts.

And, to my amazement, they work. They work because the color comes from the designs and logos on the T-shirts. But I don't think that this quilt would have worked as well if there had been just one or two colored T-shirts while the rest were white. The colored T-shirts would have stood out and distracted from the other T-shirts.

All White T-shirt Quilt

Next, you need to consider each T-shirt individually and ask questions about each T-shirt. These questions are about how each T-shirt will be seen as part of the whole of the quilt. There are no right or wrong answers to these questions. But you do need to consider how the quilt will be used now and over the generations.

1. Is the T-shirt stained, ripped or raggedy? If so, will the rip or stain be inside or outside the cutting area? If it is inside the cutting area, is this area going to be noticeable on the quilt? Can the torn area be repaired?

A ripped T-shirt

How important is the T-shirt? T-shirts that have stains or rips can be used, but you have to be able to live with the way they look in the quilt. (In Chapter 4 there is more information about working with ripped T-shirts.)

2. Does the subject content of the T-shirt match that of the other T-shirts? For example, you have 20 vacation T-shirts and one T-shirt from a 5K run – will this one race T-shirt work with the vacation T-shirts? It may or may not work. Remember, once the T-shirt is in the quilt, it is always there.

3. Will the T-shirt look out of place with the other T-shirts? For example, you have one homemade T-shirt in with a grouping of T-shirts from a person's childhood. A homemade T-shirt is one that has been made by drawing or writing on a plain T-shirt with a permanent maker or paint. How will this look? It is a hard call, but again it is your call. I have found from experience that just one homemade T-shirt may look out of place, but if there is more than one, the mix will most likely work. One issue with homemade T-shirts is they tend to be large and they may look out of proportion to the other T-shirts. Keep this in mind when making your choice of T-shirts.

4. Will a particular T-shirt keep the quilt owner from using the quilt? This is an important question no matter who you are making a quilt for. For example, if the quilt is for a guy graduating from high school and you put a T-shirt in from his childhood, will this embarrass him to the point that he will not use the quilt? It has happened.

5. Is the T-shirt appropriate? Let's face it, some high school guys just have some vulgar T-shirts. A T-shirt with *Make 7* on the front and *Up Yours* on the back may be cool now, but will it be in 20 years *(Make 7-Up Yours)*? Will this person want his or her children to see these types of T-shirts? This is a question that goes to the use of the quilt and who will see it over its life.

6. In the years to come, will the printing deteriorate or the appliqués fall off? Homemade appliqué items, if not well made, tend to fall off easily. Iron-on letters also tend to fall off. Some commercially printed

Cracked and faded printing

T-shirts have shorter lives than others. If the printing is starting to come off now, it will continue to peal off in the future. There is also commercial printing of a thick plastic type ink. Sometimes this also does not hold up over time.

7. Will you remember the meaning of the T-shirt in 20 years? Some T-shirts have sayings on them that mean something now, but will you remember the meaning of them in the future? Will someone in 80 years understand the meaning of the saying?

8. Is the T-shirt a duplicate of one already in the quilt? This doesn't preclude using this T-shirt, but you should give it some additional thought. I have found that in smaller quilts a duplicate T-shirt stands out. But in a larger quilt with 40 or 50 T-shirts, it may be hard to pick out the duplicate. However, if the T-shirt is of a unique color or design, it may stand out in any size quilt.

Only T-shirts?

As you gather T-shirts, you might find other items that you would like to include in your quilt. Many items can be used. Listed below are some items that I have used:

- Bandanas
- Baseball jerseys & uniforms
- Jog bras
- Towels - golf, fan or beach
- Patches
- Pants
- Pockets
- Sweat shirts or pants

- Bike jerseys
- Hockey jerseys & other mesh shirts
- Baby bibs
- Tank tops or sleeveless shirts
- Socks
- Gloves or mittens
- Baby blankets
- Gymnastic outfits

- Swimsuits
- Nylon running shorts/tops
- Bags
- Nylon warmup coats
- Ballet skirts
- Knit sweaters
- Vests
- Baby or Kids clothes

Some of these items, like gloves and socks, are sewn onto a spare piece of T-shirt material. Others are backed by a spare piece of T-shirt material. As a general rule, something will work well in a T-shirt quilt if it is stretchy like T-shirt material. Sewing will be a little more tricky when the item is too stretchy as compared to T-shirt material or when it is not as stretchy as T-shirt material. In Chapter 4, *Cutting Non-Standard T-shirts*, there are directions on how to work with some of these items.

A graduation gown is usable but not washable

Another consideration is the washability of the items you include in the quilt. Can it be washed like you would a T-shirt? Will the color run or bleed? T-shirt quilts are easily washed in a washing machine so a *Dry Clean Only* item should not be included unless you always plan to dry clean the quilt.

For your first quilt, I would suggest that you stick to just everyday normal T-shirts because it will be easier to get the knack of making this type of quilt with them.

Preparing the T-shirts for the Quilt

Begin by washing and drying all the T-shirts together. This goes against all the rules about sorting laundry into darks, lights and colors. But, when the quilt is made, all the T-shirts will be washed together anyway, so do it now. If you are worried that some colored T-shirts (like the red ones) will run, test them before you mix them with the other T-shirts in the washing machine.

If you find you have a "runny" T-shirt, you will need to set the dye. This can be done by soaking the T-shirt(s) in cold water and white vinegar. Set the washing machine on the soak cycle and add about a cup of the white vinegar and let the item soak over night. Rinse out the vinegar in the morning. Then wash the item(s) with your normal laundry detergent. In this load of laundry, put in a Shout® Color Catcher sheet. When you pull the items out of the washing machine, check your Color Catcher sheet to see if it is bright red (or the color of

Shout® Color Catcher

your T-shirts) or white. If it is white, the color should be set. If it is not, wash the T-shirts again with a few more Color Catchers. When they come out white, your color should be set. If the color still bleeds, try soaking in white vinegar again. And if it again does not set, then discard this T-shirt. But, most of the time, T-shirts are well worn and have been washed many times.

Dry the T-shirts as you normally would. When the T-shirts are dry, pull them out and lay them flat, one on top of the other. You could just toss them in a basket, but smooth, unwrinkled T-shirts are easier to work with.

Now, it's time to get ready to cut your T-shirts. I like doing this part the best because it is fun and easy. But do read the next section before you begin and take your time.

College Graduation/Sorority T-shirt Quilt

Chapter 3

Cutting Standard T-shirts

Now that all your T-shirts are gathered and clean, it is time to cut them. You may find it difficult to cut a T-shirt that is still perfectly good. But cutting the T-shirts can be one of the most enjoyable parts of the process. Yes, the first cut can be difficult, but once you get past the "Agh… I can't cut this T-shirt, it's still good!" the fun will begin. Simply view the process as making a quilt and a bundle of rags. (And rags you will have!)

Tools
- Large rotary cutting mat – 30" x 36"
- Small rotary cutting mat – 18" x 24"
- Rotary cutter – with a new blade
- Cutting templates – purchased or homemade (instructions below)
- 3" x 30" rotary cutting ruler
- Small straight pins
- Scissors
- Fine point Sharpie®-type marking pen

Basis of the Quilt
The T-shirt quilts described in this book are based on a 4" square. The final dimensions of each block must be divisible by 4.

For example, a block that is 16" x 12" is made up of four 4" units wide by three 4" units down. Having the quilt based on a 4" square makes it possible to cut many different sized T-shirt blocks and piece 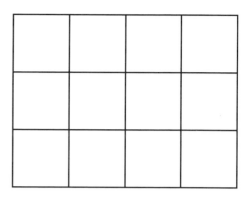 them together into a single quilt. Since there are many possible block sizes, every T-shirt can be cut so the block fits the design on the T-shirt. The system is flexible and the math is easy.

Making Cutting Templates

If you have not purchased a set of cutting templates from Too Cool T-shirt Quilts, you will need to make a set or contact us to purchase a set at www.TooCoolTshirtQuilts.com. You can make a set of cutting templates out of a clear plastic acrylic such as Plexiglas®. Making them is easier and less expensive than you might think. It involves a trip to a local hardware or home improvement store and about $30. I went to a local hardware store to purchase and have my Plexiglas® cut. A clerk cut the Plexiglas® as I instructed him. It took about 15 minutes. The Plexiglas® itself should cost less than $30 and the store may cut it for free.

If you can't find anyone at a hardware store to cut your templates, you can cut the Plexiglas® yourself. If you cut it yourself you will need a metal straight edge, two spring clamps or masking tape, and a box cutter with a new blade. You will follow the same cutting steps described below.

To make your cuts, line up your straight edge on the cutting line and either clamp it or tape it in place so it will not move. Then score along the straight edge four or five times. Next remove the straight edge. Then line up the scored line over the edge of a table that has a sharp edge. Then press down onto the side of the Plexiglas® on the table and use your other hand to press down on the side hanging over the table. To break the Plexiglas® you need to press down on the overhanging section in a hard fast motion to snap it off of the main piece. If you are cutting your own Plexiglas® you need to measure very accurately. Measure twice so you only have to cut once.

Below are two guides for having the templates cut.

Template Layout Overview

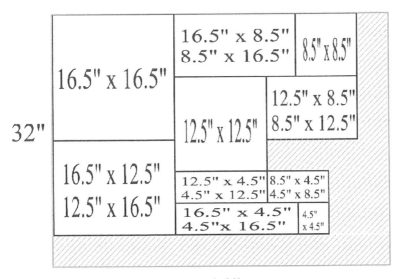

The first guide shows how the templates are laid out on the large piece of Plexiglas®. This is to give you an idea about where each template will be cut from the larger piece of Plexiglas® – it is an overview. Also note that the six rectangular templates will be used to cut two blocks – one tall by wide and the other wide by tall, thus the two sets of measurement on the guide.

The second guide (right) illustrates the step-by-step cutting progression. You should take both of these guides with you to the hardware store. In each section, the cut(s) that need to be made are illustrated. For example, in section one the first cut is a 16½" strip cut off the 32" side of the piece of Plexiglas®. The piece cut off will measure 16½" x 32". The remaining piece will be 27½" x 32". The next section shows the next three cuts. The waste is marked in stripes.

It is important to remember that each template needs to be the cutting size and not the final size. For example, a block with a final size of 16" x 16" needs to be cut with seam allowances. The seam allowance is ¼" on each side. So, the actual dimensions of the template and block would be 16½" x 16½". The template sizes shown in the cutting guides include your seam allowance.

Template Cut-by-Cut Instructions

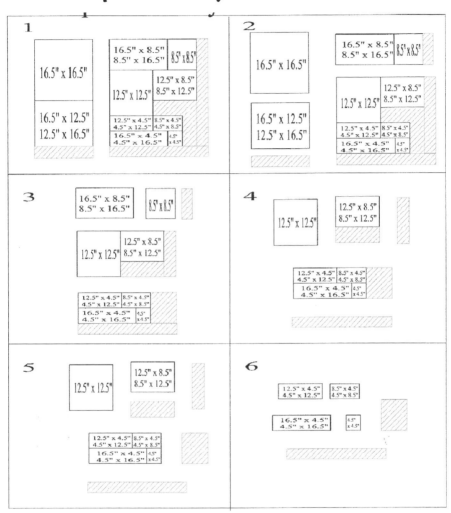

After your templates are made you can make the guides on the Plexiglas® templates with a black fine point Sharpie®. Items to mark on the templates are the template size, the center point and the ¼" seam allowance. Use your commercial ruler to mark the seam allowance and center lines. Note that the six rectangular templates will be used for two blocks – one tall by wide and the other wide by tall.

Template Marking Instructions

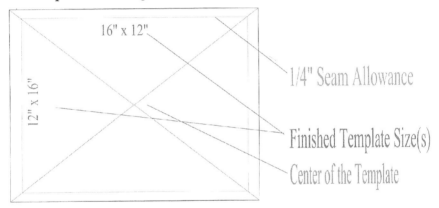

16" x 12"

12" x 16"

1/4" Seam Allowance

Finished Template Size(s)
Center of the Template

Getting Started

Before starting, review the instructions presented below, then practice. Choose an old beat-up T-shirt that will not be used in the quilt to practice cutting on. Use the smaller templates and cut a number of blocks of various sizes from this T-shirt. If necessary, practice on additional T-shirts until you feel comfortable with the process. Save these blocks that you practiced cutting to use later when practicing sewing techniques.

As you are cutting, remember to use care with the rotary cutter. It's a good idea to install a new blade in your rotary cutter before you begin. A new blade will make cutting easier, safer and reduces the chance of the template moving while you are cutting. When you use a dull blade, you have to push on the rotary cutter too hard, which may cause the template to slip and the block to be miss-cut. Also, a new blade reduces the chance of cutting yourself and, if you are cut, at least it will be a cleaner cut. Just be careful. A new cutting blade is safer and easier to work with.

Here are some other rotary cutting safety tips: Only open the safety immediately before you cut. Close the safety as soon as you finish cutting – do not lay the rotary cutter down until the safety has been closed. Watch your fingers. Also watch your wrist. I have not cut my fingers, but I have nicked my wrist. This happened when I was moving too fast while cutting along the left and top sides of the template without moving to the other side of the table. While you are moving T-shirts, cutting mats and templates around, be careful not to knock the rotary cutter off of the table.

The Grain of a T-shirt

Just like any fabric, T-shirt material has a grain. Generally, the grain runs from top to bottom of the T-shirt. When a T-shirt is cut with the grain skewed, it is more difficult to work with. But, the reality of T-shirts is that there are T-shirts that are printed crooked to the grain or the T-shirt was made with little regard to the grain.

Most of the time, you will want to or need to use these T-shirts. Sometimes you can compensate for the skewed grain by cutting the T-shirt a little crooked to the printing while lining up the template.

The left photograph shows a T-shirt with skewed grain when compared to the design on the shirt. The line in the photographs shows the direction the grain is going. On this T-shirt, the design was printed visually correct on the T-shirt, but it crosses the grain as seen by lining the template up with the printing. In the right photograph, the template is lined up with the grain of the T-shirt. As you can see, the design is not lined up in the template.

Basic T-shirt Cutting

Slip a mat into the T-shirt

First, place the large cutting mat on a table. Occasionally this mat will be used for cutting but, most of the time, it is there to keep your table from being damaged by a stray rotary cut. Next, slip the small mat into a T-shirt and lay it on top of the large cutting mat. The cutting mat is placed inside the T-shirt so that the back of the T-shirt is not cut when you cut the front. It also allows you to smooth out one side of the T-shirt without having to worry about the back.

Once the T-shirt is in place and laying flat, choose a template and place it on top of the T-shirt. Then check the size of the template to the design.

When does a template fit the design on the T-shirt? First, the entire design, or the part of the design you want, fits within the template with at least ¼" seam allowance around the design. Having more space around the design is better than having the

Template on a T-shirt

design almost cut off. Just as margins are visually important in books, so is having a margin around the design on a block. Here are some questions to ask about the alignment of the template: Is the design centered in the square? Does the design look pleasing? When you are happy with the placement of the template, it is time to cut the T-shirt.

To cut the block out, place one hand on the template and press straight down. Make sure the template does not slip or slide. Cut along all four sides. Be sure to cut past each corner a ¼" so the block is completely cut out. It may be necessary for you to move around to other sides of the table to cut the left and top sides of the template.

When positioning the rotary cutter to cut along the template, move the blade toward the template from the side until it touches the template. Then move the cutter backward along the edge of the template until the blade is just at the corner of the block. The blade is not cutting the fabric while it is being positioned; rather it is just skimming the top of the fabric. If you try to line up the blade with the template below the corner, there is the chance that the blade will run into the template when you cut. This makes an awful crunching noise and dulls your rotary cutter.

After cutting, close and set aside the rotary cutter and lift the fabric around the template to make sure the block is free of the T-shirt. If you have missed cutting a spot, the template will still be in place so you can easily cut that spot again. Finally, remove the template and pick up the block.

If there is anything on the back of the T-shirt that needs to be cut out, flip the T-shirt and the

A cut T-shirt block free of the surrounding material

board over together and cut the back side by following the same steps as outlined above. If not, slip the small cutting mat out of the T-shirt and go on to the next T-shirt.

> **Hint:** There are some instances in which you may not remember what was the top or bottom of the T-shirt block you cut. For example, did you cut a 9 or a 6? Instead of trying to remember, make a mark within the ¼" seam allowance on the top side of the block with either a straight pin or a marking pen

As you cut the blocks from the T-shirts, it helps to stack them into like-sized piles. This will help in the next step – counting the blocks. As you are stacking remember that you will have two piles of blocks for each rectangular template. For example, you will have a pile of 12" x 16" and a pile of 16" x 12". Stacking the blocks as you cut also will give you an idea if there are too many of one size block. Typically, this will happen with 12" x 12" blocks. If you find you are getting an inordinate number of blocks, start using a size larger template to cut some additional blocks. For example, if you have too many 12" x 12" blocks, cut additional T-shirts using either the 12" x 16" or 16" x 12".

Continue cutting until the entire stack of T-shirts has been cut into blocks and rags. Sounds easy enough, but not all of the T-shirts in your stack will be this straight-forward to cut. The next chapter describes how to cut several types of non-standard T-shirts.

David's Everything Else T-shirt Quilt

Chapter 4

Cutting Non-standard T-shirts

The previous chapter described how to cut a typical or normal T-shirt. But not all T-shirts are as easy and straight-forward to cut. For example, some T-shirts have pockets while others have printing down the sleeves. Using T-shirts in your quilt that have unique and interesting items or printing will make your quilt more dynamic and exciting. This chapter provides instructions for cutting non-standard types of T-shirts. Some T-shirts will require a combination of the techniques described here. Other T-shirts may not quite fit any of the techniques and may require a creative solution for cutting.

Tools

- Large rotary cutting mat – 30" x 36"
- Small rotary cutting mat – 18" x 24"
- Rotary cutter – with a new blade
- Cutting templates
- 3" x 30" rotary cutting ruler
- Small straight pins
- Scissors
- Fine point Sharpie®-type marking pen
- Fray Check™

Pinning a Backing Piece to a Block

Many non-standard T-shirts require a blank block of T-shirt material be pinned behind it. Some examples are when your T-shirt is very thin, mesh, has a hole in it, or the T-shirt needs additional fabric. A blank block is cut from scrap T-shirt material and is the same size as the top block. After both blocks have been cut out they are pinned together.

When pinning the blocks together, the grain of each block should run the same direction under most circumstances. The one instance when the grains should be at a 90 degree angle to each other is when the top block is very stretchy.

To pin the blank block to the top block, line up one corner on each piece and pin the two together in the corner within the seam allowance. The pins used should be small and sharp as to minimize holes. Pin the three other corners in this same fashion. Do not worry about lining up the sides. After all four corners have been pinned, the block should line up itself. It may need to be shaken a little to line up. If not, line it up when sewing it into the quilt. They will be sewn into the quilt as if they are one block.

 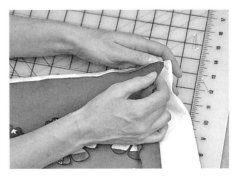

 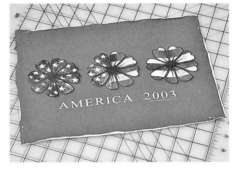

Pinning a blank block to a T-shirt block:
    Top Left: A T-shirt block and blank block
    Top Right: Lining up two corners
    Bottom Left: A corner pinned
    Bottom Right: All four corners pinned

Breast Pockets

Having a pocket on a T-shirt quilt is a lot of fun. It is one of the blocks people comment on most when seeing a quilt for the first time. Some T-shirts with pockets will have printing on them and others do not. Even if a pocket does not have anything printed on it, a bright colored pocket will add interest to your quilt.

To cut out the pocket, center the template over the pocket, press down on the template and cut. Be prepared for the template to wobble. The template may wobble because it is resting on the pocket which is on top of the material; therefore, the template is raised off of the cutting surface.

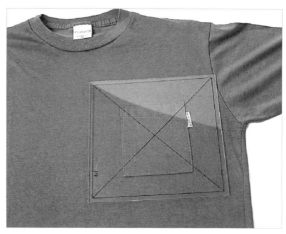

T-shirt with pocket under a template.

There are two options if the template is rocking too much to easily cut around or if the template is so high off the cutting mat that the hub on the rotary cutter hits the template and prevents the blade from cutting. The first option is to rock the template down toward the side to be cut before cutting that side. Rock it down toward the side to be cut, make the cut and rock it back up. Repeat for each side. The other option is to mark the cutting lines with a pen and cut with scissors. To do this, line up the template and trace it with a fabric pen. Then remove the cutting board and cut the block out with scissors.

Pouch-Type Pockets

Most hooded sweatshirts have pouch-type pockets. Although most pouch-type pockets do not have printing on them, many do have printing above them. Sometimes in order to fit the printing above the pocket within the area of a template requires including some of the pocket under the template. To add texture and interest to your quilt, consider adding the pocket along with the printing above it.

To cut out the pouch pocket, begin by lining up the template. The bottom edge of the template should be above the bottom seam

Pouch pocket with printing above it

of the pocket. If you were to include the ribbing in the quilt, you may have problems with the stretch when sewing because the ribbing will stretch differently than the sweatshirt material. Ribbing is designed to gather in fabric thereby taking a wide amount of fabric and making it narrow. Thus, the seam between ribbing and sweatshirt is thick and would be lumpy in the final quilt. So cut off the bottom ribbing with your scissors.

A template lined up over the pouch pocket — the bottom ribbing is being cut off

After realigning the template, cut as normal. Since many layers of fabric may need to be cut along the bottom, more than one pass with the cutter may be necessary. In the final seam, at least two layers of fabric from the sweatshirt will be sewn into the seam – the sweatshirt and the pocket.

Collars and Necklines

Sometimes to be able to fit the entire design on the T-shirt into the area of the template, more material is needed than is available. This does not prevent the T-shirt from being used; it just means that the block will need to

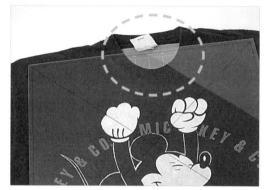

A template extending over the neck line of a T-shirt

be extended. The process is to cut the T-shirt as if the material is there and then fill in the missing material with a blank block cut from scrap T-shirt material. Complete directions for various types of necklines are below.

Scoop Neck Collars – On some T-shirts the printing extends up beyond the lowest part of the neckline. In order to fit all the printing within the template, the template must over the neckline of the T-shirt. In this situation, set the T-shirt to cut as normal, but cut through the neckline as if it were there. Then cut a scrap of T-shirt material larger than the open neckline. This can be in a matching or a contrasting color. Then place the scrap T-shirt material behind the top block and pin the two together around the neck area. Next, sew around the ribbing of the collar where it meets the T-shirt with a straight stitch in a matching thread. Last, trim the scrap material to within a quarter inch of the seam.

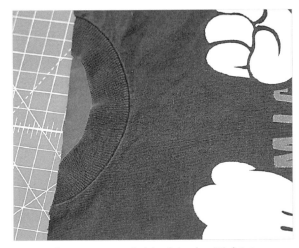

Scrap material behind a T-shirt block with a scoop neck

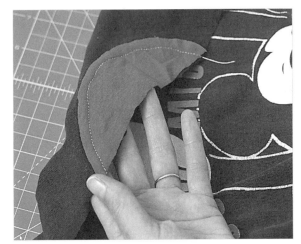

Scrap material behind a T-shirt block sewn down and trimmed

Polo-Type T-shirt – Polo-type shirts typically have printing or embroidery stitching on the upper left-hand chest. Sometimes, to get the design centered under the template, the template has to overlap the buttons and collar. Including a block that has an actual piece of collar and the buttons in the quilt is fun and reminds people that this quilt was made from shirts.

To cut out these blocks, begin by preparing to cut the shirt as normal. Button up the shirt and smooth it out with the small cutting mat inside. Then smooth the collar into place. When the template is placed on the shirt, make sure it is not in a position in which a button will be cut through. As with other collared shirts, part of the template may not have fabric under it if the template extends up over the neckline. Cut the block out as normal.

It may be difficult cutting through the collar and neckline. The multiple layers of fabric and the thick collar pieces may make multiple passes necessary. The more passes required with the rotary cutter increases the likelihood that the template may slip. Begin by cutting the three sides of the block that do not include the collar and cut the collar side last. If you are concerned with the possible difficulty of cutting through the collar, mark the last side of the block with a fabric marking pen, pin down the collar and then cut with scissors.

Left: The marked cutting line on a thick area of a T-shirt
Right: Cutting the thick area with scissors

After cutting, carefully lift up the template and pin the loose collar pieces into place. Most of the time, the collar will still be attached to the block. But they should be pinned down at this time anyway. Pinning the collar into place will ensure that the ends

Pin down collar pieces within the seam allowance

of the collar will be in the correct position and not cockeyed.

Next, if there is missing material, pin a blank block behind the top block. Smooth out the two blocks together. Last, with a straight stitch, sew down the shirt opening with matching thread. After sewing the shirt opening, tack down the top edge of the collar pieces within the ¼" seam allowance.

Hooded Sweatshirts with Strings – The neckline from hooded sweatshirts that includes the hood strings can also add fun to your quilt. It is also a reminder of what the shirt was when it was worn. Cutting these shirts is very similar to cutting other shirts with collars.

Begin by inserting the cutting board into the shirt. Pull the shirt down so shoulder seams are over the top of the board. Smooth out the shirt with the hood strings hanging out of the shirt. If the strings are too short, cut the center of the hood through the strings with a pair of scissors. Gently pull out the hood strings to the desired length. Then pin the strings through the hood above the template so they do not accidentally come out of the holes or grommets while working with the shirt.

Next, position the template so the top is at least ¾" above the string grommet holes. This ensures that the grommet holes

will show on the block and not be lost in the seam allowance. Check that the strings are under the template before you begin cutting. As with other nonstandard T-shirts, the template may not lay flat and

String hang from a hooded sweatshirt in a T-shirt quilt

may rock or slip while the block is being cut. Cut the block out. Pin down the loose hood strings within the ¼" seam allowance.

After cutting out the block, if there is missing material, pin a blank block on the back. If a neckline needs to be sewn down, do so. Also sew down, within the ¼" seam allowance, the loose hood strings that were previously pinned down. To keep the hood strings that are sewn down within the seam allowance from fraying, put a drop of Fray Check™ on the cut ends. If the ends hanging on the outside of the shirt are frayed put Fray Check™ on the knot of the strings. This will allow the bottoms to continue to fray without the entire string fraying.

When sewing blocks with hood strings into the quilt, be careful with the free strings while sewing so they do not get sewn into the seam. Also, a shirt block with strings should not be placed on the top row of the quilt because the grommet holes may get lost in the binding.

If your hoodie has a neckline that is too far above the printing to look good, you can use the strings without including the neck line. First cut the strings through the center of the hood. Pull each string out and pin a length of each to the top of the cut block. Then sew each string down within the seam allowance as directed above.

T-shirts With Printing Larger than Largest Template

Designs on most T-shirts will fit within the 16" x 16" template. But there are some T-shirts that have oversized designs. These are great to use in quilts. But beyond cutting considerations, the proportion of the block to all of the other blocks in the quilt and the placement of the block within the quilt need to be considered. If the cut block is very large and the quilt is small, this one block will dominate the quilt. But if the quilt is large, a large block will most likely blend in well.

The positioning of the large block will also influence how well it works within a quilt. Since most large blocks are placed on the outside of the quilt, the placement helps the blocks from over powering the smaller blocks. If a large block is placed in the center of the quilt, the block becomes more dominate. If it is an important

T-shirt, placing it in the center may work. If it has less sentimental value, a center placement may not be desirable.

T-shirts with large designs take more preparation and consideration than a standard T-shirt. Think through the cutting process before you begin cutting. T-shirts with large designs are

cut without the small cutting mat. Therefore, if the T-shirt has printing on the front and back it will need to be cut open, usually along the side seams, before it is laid out.

A T-shirt with oversize design laid out with 2 templates to make a block that is 24" x 16"

To cut open a T-shirt, cut the side seams

from the bottom up to the armpit and down the under arm seam. Choose the side to cut that will cut off the least printing. Next, cut both sleeves along the shoulder seams though the neckline. Be sure to cut down the *top* of the sleeve; otherwise

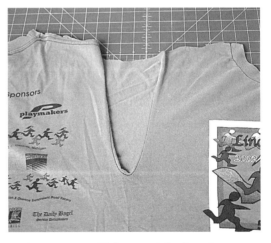

A cutopen T-shirt with the sleeve tucked under itself

you will lose the use of the material from the armpit area. Once you have cut the T-shirt open, spread it out across a large cutting mat. To lay the sleeve out, fold the sleeve under itself.

T-shirts with designs larger than the 16" x 16" will require using multiple templates to make one large template. Begin by placing the largest template that fits the design in the upper left-hand corner of the design. Then add other templates until the entire design is covered. Note: Overlap each template by ½" or the final block will be too big. To do this, line up the overlapping templates so that the ¼" mark on one template is on top of the ¼" mark on the other. The overlap is to compensate for the seam allowance that is built into the templates.

Oversize blocks are cut as normal with one exception: the overlapped sections. Be careful when approaching the overlap of the templates with your rotary cutter because they do not stay perfectly lined up. They will move just enough out of place so that if

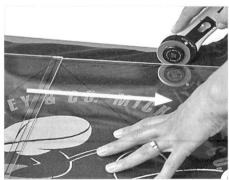

Top — The starting position for the rotary cutter

Bottom — The first cut is backward and the final cut is forward from the template overlap you cut from one template to the other, your rotary cutter blade will run into the template. This dulls the rotary cutter and makes an awful sound. So, start cutting at the overlap and cut down on one template and then go back to the overlap and cut up on that template. Hold down each template individually while cutting.

The last thing to do is note the size of the T-shirt block because you may not remember it later and then will have to measure it again.

T-shirts With Wrap-Around Printing

T-shirts with printing that wraps around the body of the T-shirt are popular. These T-shirts are suitable for use in your quilt. Remember to think about the size of the block in relationship to the other blocks. Cutting these T-shirts are very similar to cutting oversized T-shirts.

Start by following the direction above for cutting T-shirts with oversize designs. Most of these types of T-shirts will have one side under an arm where the design begins and ends. Cut up the side and down

Top - A T-shirt with printing wrap-around the entire T-shirt

Bottom - Cutting up through under arm

the underarm of the T-shirt where the design begins and ends. Next, cut the shoulder seams open. After the T-shirt has been cut open, lay the T-shirt out flat. If the templates lay over the armpit of the T-shirt, fold and tuck the arm so it lies smoothly.

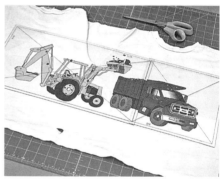

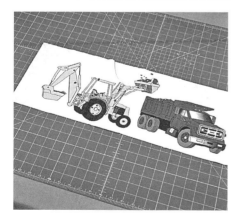

Top Left - Cut up top of arm through the neck

Top Right - Cut from the neck down the other arm

Middle Left- Cut open and ready to tuck the sleeve under

Middle Right - Lay out the templates

Left - Cut out of the T-shirt

Next, lay out the template(s) as described in the section about cutting large T-shirts on page 44. Cut the T-shirt and carefully remove the templates. Pin down the armpit as it was folded when it was cut. Then sew along the armpit seam with a straight stitch in matching thread. Finally, trim the excess material from behind the armpit.

Sleeves – Long and Short

Some T-shirts have printing on their sleeves which you can use in your quilt. To use a sleeve, cut the sleeve off at the shoulder. If there is a cuff made with ribbing, cut it off just above the ribbing. Then cut along the inside seam of the sleeve, flatten it

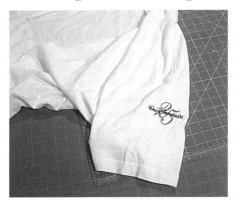

Top Left - T-shirt with printing on the sleeve

Top Right - Sleeve cut off of T-shirt

Left - sleeve cut open and laid flat

out, and cut the block as normal. Last, if necessary, mark the top of the sleeve block with a mark within the seam allowance with a Sharpie® because sometimes the printing is such that you may not remember what was the top or the bottom of the block.

T-shirts With Non-Flat Items

T-shirts with unique items can add pizzazz to your quilt. Generally, these can be cut as normal, except that the template might rock with these items under it.

The bows on two of the dogs are real bows

There are two options if the template is rocking too much to easily cut around it or if the template is so high off of the cutting mat that the rotary cutter's hub hits the template and prevents the blade from being able to cut. The first option is to rock the template down towards the side to be cut before cutting that side. Rock it down towards the side to be cut, make the cut and rock it back up. Repeat for each side. The other option is to mark the cutting lines with a pen and cut with scissors. To do this, line up the template and trace it with a fabric pen. Then remove the cutting board and cut the block out with scissors.

Thin T-shirts, Mesh T-shirts and T-shirts With Holes

Some T-shirts are just old, worn and thin. Some even have holes in them. And some are mesh which is all holes. These T-shirts can be used in your quilt if they are backed with another piece of T-shirt material.

Begin by cutting out the T-shirts as normal. Then cut out a blank block from scrap T-shirt material. Check the color of the scrap material with the T-shirt block over it. For mesh T-shirts, try a variety of colors to see what looks best through the holes. Sometimes a contrasting color looks better than a matching color. Last, pin the two blocks together at the four corners as instructed earlier on page 35. They will be sewn together when the quilt is pieced.

Left - Cut mesh T-shirt as normal
Right - Red backing material on the left, white on the right

If the hole or rip in the T-shirt is larger than a nickle, zigzag in matching thread around the hole. If the hole is small, don't zigzag. Whether it is a large or small hole, put Fray Check™ around the hole to keep it from enlarging.

Not Enough Material – General Solution

There are some items that you might like to use in your quilt that do not have enough material to fill an entire template. Some examples are a tank top, swimsuit, patches, small line of type from a T-shirt, or anything else that is washable that you might like to use. These items are mounted onto blank blocks of T-shirt material and then sewn down before the block is put into the quilt. Below are some examples with a brief description of how to approach the problem.

Patches

Patches are easy - just center the patch on a blank block or another block and then straight stitch around it just inside the satin stitching that goes around the patch. I sew there because it is least visible.

Baseball Caps

Everyone seems to have baseball caps and think that they should go into a T-shirt quilt. But, as you know, baseball caps are not flat. However, since I have so many requests to use them, I figured out how to incorporate them. Cut around the saying or logo on the cap and sew it onto a blank block just as you would a patch except that you should zigzag around the piece.

Tank Tops

First cut the top out as if it had all the material you need (right). Then cut a blank block with the same template. Pin the cut tank top to the blank block and then straight  stitch along each arm hole just inside the binding. Trim off the excess fabric to within ¼" of the seam.

Already Cut T-shirts

Sometimes you inherit T-shirts that someone has started to make a quilt with and then decided after cutting them that they 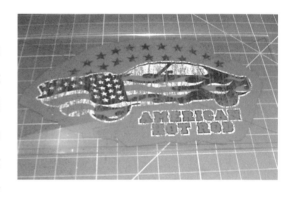 had no idea what to do with the blocks. I have been given some very messed-up pieces of T-shirt blocks that either didn't fit in a template and/ or were cut with a pair of kitchen scissors. These blocks are not difficult to use. If the piece can be cut with a template, just cut it like a standard block. If not, mount the piece of block onto a blank block of a matching color. Sometimes the pre-cut block will partly fit under the template. In this case, lay down the blank block and place the messed-up block on top of it.

You may need to trim one or two sides of the pre-cut block that overhangs the blank block. Once the block is pinned to the blank block, zigzag around the block in matching thread.

Towels, Blankets, Bandanas and Scarves

Towels, blankets, bandanas and scarves can all be used as whole block backed with another piece of T-shirt material.

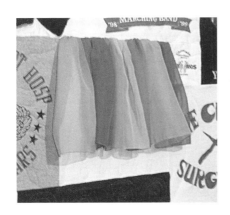

But you also might choose to just use a corner of the material for a more dynamic look. The picture (left) shows the use of a silky-type dress scarf. To do this, first cut a blank in a contrasting color. Next, gather the scarf using a basting stitch along one side of the scarf on a sewing machine. Pull one thread to gather the material. Then pin the scarf to the blank block. ten to 20 pins might be needed. Stitch the scarf to the blank block on the gathered side within the seam allowance. Last, sew the two sides to the blank block, again within the seam allowance. Sewing within the seam allowance means that the stitches will not show up on the quilt top - they

are hidden inside the seam allowance.

To use the corner of a bandana or a towel, first cut a blank block. Then lay the item so the corner is about an inch from the seam. You can lay the corner on point as it is in the photograph to the left or you can line the corner up to the corner of the blank block, leaving about an inch of the blank block showing. Place the template back on the blank block and bandana and trim the excess bandana off. Next, pin the bandana to the blank block. Last, stitch the bandana down to the blank block using a straight stitch in a matching thread.

Outfits - Baby or Otherwise

Dance outfits and baby dresses are cute enough that you might want to use the entire front of the outfit. First, cut a blank block that is larger than the item you want to mount. Next, lay

the outfit on the blank block and note its edges. You need to cut the back of the outfit off leaving about ½" of material that can be folded back under the dress. Then pin the outfit down, folding under the excess material. Last, sew around the outfit with a straight stitch in matching thread.

Boxer Shorts

Boxer shorts are an old stand-by for most high school kids. To use these you can just take a block of material which could even include the fly. If you want to include the waist band, start by cutting open the shorts. Cut the two crotch seams first. Then choose which other seam you want to cut. It could be a side seam or the rear seam. Next, determine what size block you need by laying a template over the cut-open shorts. Be sure to have the template extend over the top of the waistline. Then cut the shorts as if they filled the entire template. Then cut a blank block. Pin the shorts to the blank block and sew with a straight stitch along the waistline of the shorts.

Only Part of the Design on the T-shirt is Wanted

There are situations where you only want to use a single line of text from the shirt or you want to remove a section of print from the part you want. To use just a small part of the

design, cut out that part and mount it on a blank block. Then zigzag around it in matching thread. If there is part of a shirt that you don't want to use, begin by cutting the block as normal. Then cut out the unwanted section. Mount this block, that now has a hole in it, to a blank block cut from the same T-shirt. Last, zigzag and Fray Check™ around the hole.

Top Left: #21 is not wanted.
Bottom Left: Part that is not wanted is cut out and sewn to a blank block.

T-shirts Without Enough Material at the Bottom

There are situations when there will not be enough material at the bottom of the T-shirt or its sleeve. Sometimes

this is because the T-shirt is small: other times it is because the design is too large for the T-shirts or because that is how it was printed.

Not enough material at the bottom

If you are short about ½" or less, the solution is simple: you unfold the hem. To do this, first lay your template on the T-shirt. Then cut up through the hem about an inch. Your cut should be made on both sides of the template about two inches away from it. Then, remove the T-shirt from the cutting mat and cut carefully with scissors along the bottom of the stitching on the hem. Last, reposition the T-shirt on the cutting mat, unfold the hem and cut as normal.

Top - About an inch from the template, cut up through the hem about an inch

Top Middle - Cut along the seam

Bottom Middle - Fold down the hem

Bottom - Turn over and cut as normal

If, including the hem, there is not enough material then you will need to add additional material at the bottom. First, cut the block out as normal. You will not have a bottom to cut because the material does not extend below the bottom of the template. Next, cut a blank block from the same T-shirt material that is the same size. Pin the two blocks together and zigzag the top block to the blank block in matching thread.

You may run into other situations that were not discussed here. Some items like socks and gloves may just need to be sewn on top of a blank piece of T-shirt material. But most of the time if you apply one or more of the methods discussed here, you should be able to determine a solution.

Grab your calculator; it is now time to get ready for the first of two steps in laying out the quilt. In this next step it is important to be very accurate. So take your time and do this slowly.

Chapter 5
Stacking and Counting

This step, stacking and counting, is the first of two steps in laying out the quilt. This step involves counting the blocks and determining the size of the quilt. Read through these directions carefully and proceed slowly – one miscounted block will throw off your entire quilt plan and will result in a recount and going through these steps again. I know the agony of a miscount, so proceed carefully.

Tools
- Photocopy of Layout Counting Chart (See Appendix i)
- Pen or pencil
- Calculator

Counting
The first step is to stack all the blocks according to their size into separate stacks. Be sure to separate out the blocks that are wider than tall from the blocks that are taller than wide. For example, there should be two stacks of blocks cut from the 12" x 16" template – those that are 12" wide and those that are 16" wide.

Blocks separated by size

Next, starting with the 16" x 16" blocks, count the number of blocks in each stack. Count again (and again if needed!) and write that number down on Layout Counting Chart in the second column labeled "# of Blocks" next to the corresponding block size on the chart. Then count the next size down, the 16" x 12" blocks.

Example – Layout Counting Chart

Block Size	# of Blocks		Square Inches		Total Square Inches
16 x 16	5	x	256	=	
16 x 12	6	x	192	=	
12 x 16	3	x	192	=	

After you count the 16" x 12" blocks, stack them on top of the 16" x 16" blocks so the bottom left-hand corners of the two stacks are aligned. Continue counting and stacking the stacks of blocks in order, working down the Layout Counting Chart until all the blocks have been counted. If there are any oversize blocks, count them and write them in on the bottom of the layout chart

in the same manner the other blocks are listed.

Blocks aligned in lower left corner and stacked with the largest blocks on the bottom and the smallest on the top

Calculating the Quilt Size

Calculating the size of your quilt requires a little math, including calculating square roots. Even if you didn't get an A in math in high school, the directions below will walk you through what you need to do. Stick with it; you have already cut your shirts!

For each block size, multiply number of blocks by the square inches on your Layout Counting Chart. The square inches is the length and width of a block multiplied together. So multiply the "# of Blocks" column by the "Square Inches" column and record that number in the "Total Square Inches" column. "Total Square Inches" represents the square inches of all the blocks of that size.

Example – Layout Counting Chart

Block Size	# of Blocks		Square Inches		Total Square Inches
16 x 16	5	x	256	=	1280
16 x 12	6	x	192	=	1152
12 x 16	3	x	192	=	576

After you have calculated the number of "Total Square Inches" for each size block, add up the "Total Square Inches" column and record this number in the "Sum of Total Square Inches" box. I usually recheck my adding at least once. The "Sum of Total Square Inches" represents the total square inches of all the blocks combined.

Example – Layout Counting Chart

Block Size	# of Blocks		Square Inches		Total Square Inches
16 x 16	5	x	256	=	**1280**
16 x 12	6	x	192	=	**1152**
12 x 16	3	x	192	=	**576**
		= Sum of Total Square Inches			**3,008**

Now take the square root of the "Sum of Total Square Inches."

$$\sqrt{3,008} = 54.84$$

This doesn't have to be calculated by hand! Most calculators have a square root function button. To figure this on the calculator, enter the "Sum of Total Square Inches" (3008) and then press the square root function key. (It looks like: $\sqrt{}$). This number represents the size quilt you could make if the quilt was a perfect square. It is a guide for determining the size of the quilt.

Now you need to play with the numbers to figure out the size of your quilt. Remember that all of the blocks in the quilt are in multiples of four inches; therefore, the length and width of the quilt each must be divisible by 4. So take the square root of "Sum of Total Square Inches" and round it down to a number divisible by 4. This becomes a possible width of the quilt.

54.84 rounds down to 52 (52÷4 = 13)

Now take the width number and divide it into the "Sum of Total Square Inches."

3,008÷52 = 57.8

The perfect length to the width of 52 would be 57.8. But this number needs to be rounded up to the next highest number that is divisible by 4 – which is 60. So the size of the quilt would be:

52" wide by 60" tall

If you don't like that size, play with the numbers. Round the "Sum of Total Square Inches" down to the next lowest number divisible by 4 and try again. So the math would be:

54.84 rounds down to 48 (48÷4 = 12)

3,008÷48 = 62.66

62.66 rounds up to 64 (64÷4 = 16)

Quilt size: 48" x 64"

Continue to do this until the quilt is the size you want. Remember the total square inches of the quilt needs to be greater than, or equal to, the square inches of the blocks. So for the example above the total square inches of the quilt is 3072. This is larger than the 3,016 square inches of blocks you have.

48 x 64 = 3,072 is greater than 3,008

What do you do if you have a larger quilt than the number of blocks as in the example above? You will use 4" x 4" squares of bright color T-shirt material to make up the missing squares. To figure out how many extra 4" x 4" blocks you need, subtract total square inches of the quilt size from the total square inches of blocks you have:

3,072 - 3,008 = 64

Divide this number by 16. The result is the number of extra 4" x 4" blocks you need.

64÷16 = 4

Now that you have established the size of your quilt, the next step is to determine where each block will go in the quilt. This will probably be the most difficult step in making your quilt but I will walk you through each step in the next chapter.

Pooh Quilt

Chapter 6

Laying Out the Quilt and Making the Map

Now you have all these different size T-shirt blocks and you know the size of the quilt you will be making. So how does it all go together? In this step you will be figuring out how all these blocks fit together into a quilt the size you want. This can be difficult and may take you some time. It may go faster if you are good at puzzles. This step involves placing your T-shirt blocks into the shape of your quilt. A representative square is used to represent each T-shirt block. You will move these representative squares around and piece the quilt together. This can be done on a computer or with graph paper. Give yourself time. And if you go crazy trying to figure this out, find someone who is good with puzzles to help you.

(I can provide help doing this step. For more information visit my web site www.TooCoolTshirtQuilts. com.)

Olivet Eagles T-shirt Quilt

The explanation of how to do this on the computer is in *Italics* and how to do this with graph paper is in **bold**.

Tools

Computer Method

- *Computer drawing or design program with the following capabilities:*
  - △ *Cut, copy and paste*
  - △ *A work space that supports a 4 inch grid*
  - △ *Print out to fit paper*
  - △ *Zoom in and out*
  - △ *Snap to grid*
- *Examples of programs*
  - △ *Auto Desk Turbo CAD™**
  - △ *MacDraft™*
- *Printer*

*If you are using Auto Desk Turbo CAD™, you can e-mail me for a copy of a pre-formatted document that you can work from at andrea@toocooltshirtquilts.com

Graph Paper Method

- **Graph paper – (many sheets)**
- **Scissors**
- **Adhesive, e.g. 505® Spray and Fix – Temporary Fabric Adhesive, tape rings, double-sided tape or glue stick**
- **Marking pens**

Representative Squares

The first step is to make a representative square to stand for each T-shirt block you cut. So if you cut 5 blocks that are 16" x 16", you will make 5 squares to represent them. Below is an example of one of each size block on a piece of graph paper.

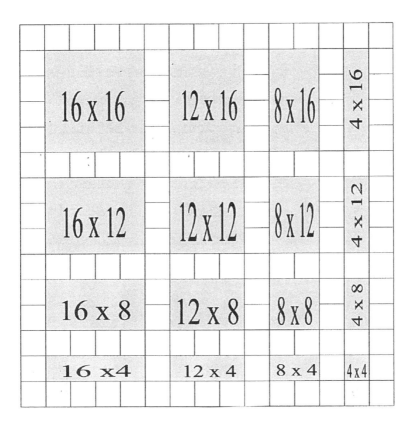

Computer

If you are unfamiliar with your program, you will need to take some time to learn its basics. If you are using Auto Desk Turbo CAD 8™ and have e-mailed me for a copy of a pre-formatted document, open up the file labeled Lay Out Master. Then SAVE AS and give it your own name.

What will open up is similar to what you see above. If you are not using Auto Desk Turbo CAD ™ you need to set the scale to a 1" = ¼" and have in the background/paper a grid in which 1 square equals 4". Next, draw a square the size of each block and type its size on it. You may have to use the Bring to Front/Send to Back feature and group the square and its typed size. Draw your arrangement so it looks like the chart above and give it a name such as "Master". Then save it again under a separate name.

For each computer represented square, copy and paste it once for each T-shirt block of that size. Paste the blocks outside the area where you will build the quilt. For example, if there are 5 blocks that are 16" x 16", copy and paste this object 4 times so there are 5 total objects that represent a 16" x 16" block. If you are using Auto Turbo 8™, you will use the rubber stamp to duplicate your squares. Right click on the square you want to duplicate, choose rubber stamp and left click for each square you need. So if you need 5 squares, left click, move the cursor and the left click again. Do this for all 5 squares and then press "escape" and "delete". Continue copying and pasting or rubber stamping until you have one square that represents each block that you cut. Then SAVE!

Graph Paper

Each square on the paper will represent 4 square inches on your quilt. So the block you cut that is 16" x 16" would be 4 squares wide by 4 squares tall. And a square that is 16" x 12" would be 4 squares wide by 3 squares tall. Start by drawing a square or rectangle on the graph paper to represent each T-shirt block you cut. If these pieces will be too small for you to work with, then have each square on your graph paper represent 2 inches on your quilt. So a block that is 16" x 16" would be 8 squares wide by 8 squares tall.

Mark each drawn square with the size of the square and number it (e.g. "1 of 4") to make sure you have all the squares. Sometimes the little pieces of paper can get lost.

After you have drawn each block, spray the back of the paper squares with 505® Spray and Fix – Temporary Fabric Adhesive. This is the preferred method for temporarily affixing the paper squares to the graph paper. However, a tape ring, a piece of double stick tape, or a dab of glue stick on the back of each cut square will also work. Then cut each block out.

While you are moving these pieces around on the paper, lightly stick them down. They will need to be pulled off and repositioned many times. But if they are not stuck down while you are laying out the quilt, they could move and mess up the design. Also, don't do this in a breezy location!

Set Outside Perimeters

Now that you have all your representative squares ready to go, you need to next set the outside perimeters of the quilt.

Computer

Use the inch markings on the ruler to see your parameters. For example if the quilt is 88" x 96" the (0", 0") is the upper left hand corner, (88", 0") is the upper right hand corner, (0", 96") is the lower left hand corner and (88", 96") is the lower right hand corner. The first number in the ( ) is the X coordinate and the second number is the Y coordinate. Move one large block into each corner so the block is on the inside of the parameter.

Graph Paper

First divide the width of the quilt by four. This is how many squares wide the quilt will be on the graph paper. If you increased each square on your graph paper to represent 2 inches on your quilt, then divide the width of the quilt by 2 to determine how many squares wide the quilt will be on the graph paper. Next, divide the length of the quilt by 4 (or 2 as per width above). This is how many squares long the quilt will be. Mark on the paper where the four corners are and then mark your corners to indicate the outside of the quilt.

Design process

The design process is the same whether you are working on the computer or with graph paper. The procedure is to arrange the squares on the graph (paper or electronic) and move them around until they all fit and make a pleasing design. Sounds easy enough, but it may take some time. Rest assured that the final quilt that is puzzled together is so cool that it is worth the time. The following are the steps I use to help build my design.

First, put a larger square in each corner. These blocks help to anchor the design. If you were to use small squares in the outside corners, they will visually fall off the quilt. Next, fill in the outside edges. Try to alternate sizes of blocks so that

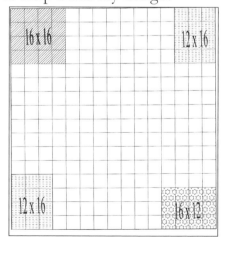

there are not all one-size blocks making up a side. Again, try to use the larger blocks first. Any block that is under 8" x 8" generally is visually too small for the outside and should be saved for the middle area.

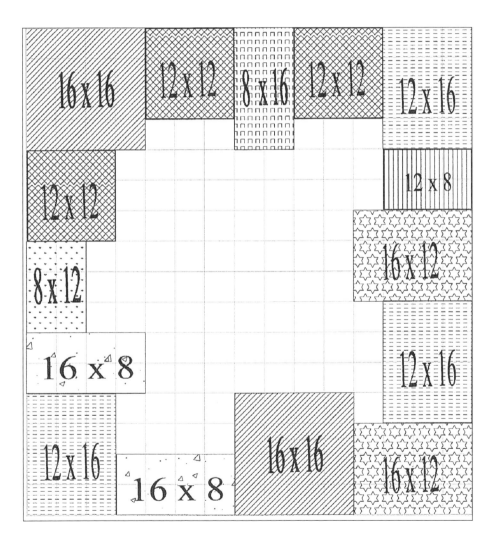

Next, fill in the interior beginning with the larger pieces. As you fill the interior, work from larger to smaller pieces. If you have a lot of 12" x 12" blocks, fill those in by off-setting one to another.

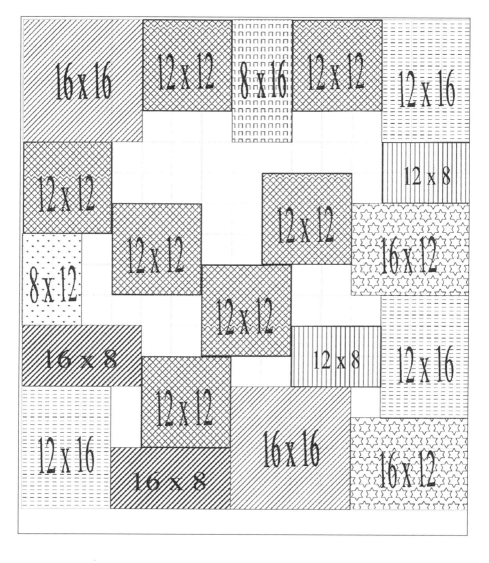

Continue to fill in blocks until the entire interior is filled.

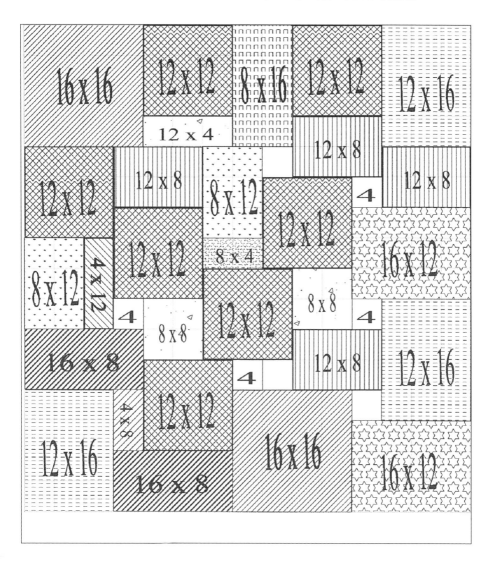

If the total square inches of your quilt is greater than the total square inches of the cut blocks, there will be open spaces. Below, the solid gray squares represent the open spaces that need to be filled with 4" blocks from colored T-shirt scraps.

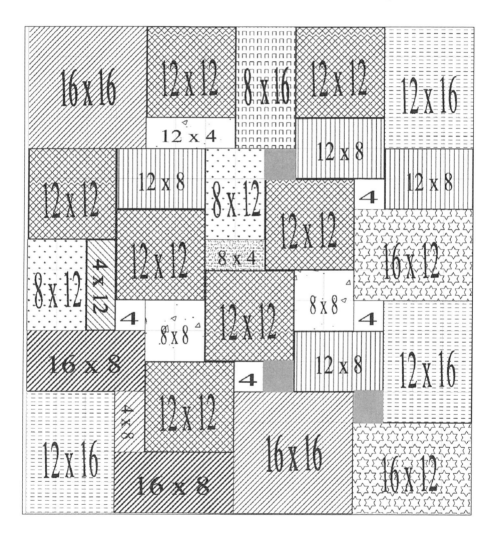

Continue rearranging the squares until you are satisfied with your design. There are a number of elements that I try to avoid because they break apart the look of the random placement of the T-shirt block. The first is avoid having four corners coming together. In the example to the left, there are two spots where 4 corners come together. To fix this, move the 12" x 8" block up and the 12" x 12" block down.

Spend some time looking at the layout to see if by moving a block or two you can eliminate four corners coming together.

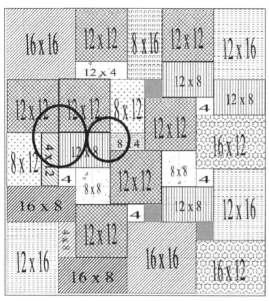

Four corners coming together

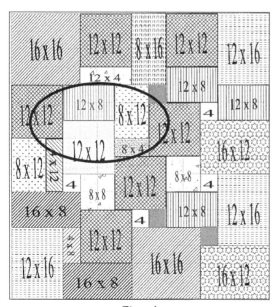

Fixed

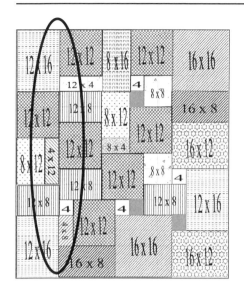

Also try to avoid a long seam from side to side or from top to bottom. This visually breaks the quilt in pieces.

The uneven distribution of blocks can also look odd. For example, all the 12" x 12" squares bunched up together throw the design off-balance.

Preparing the Final Map

When you are satisfied with your design, you will need to make a final copy to work from.

Computer

Print the drawing out onto 8 ½" x 11" white paper. To do this, you will need to tell the computer to "fit to paper" so the entire drawing fits onto one piece of paper. Go to print preview before you print to make sure it looks like what you want it to look like.

Graph Paper

Redraw your map from your final draft onto a new piece of graph paper. You need to do this so the pieces don't fall off later and because the next step involves additional drawing on the final map. It will be easier if it is on one piece of paper.

If you are completely stuck, I can do this step for you. Visit my web site at www.toocooltshirtquilts.com and click on the "Make it Yourself" link for pricing and information.

Congratulations! You have made it through the toughest part of this project! The next step in the layout process is to decide where each block will go, which is much easier and more fun.

Idea: Make a historical record of your quilt by writing about each T-shirt in the quilt. First make a photocopy of your map and number each block. Then write the history and or memory about each block. Number each note to correspond to each block.

A Little Bit of Everything T-shirt Quilt

Chapter 7

T-shirt Block
Placement on Map

Now that your map is complete, the next step is to decide where to place each T-shirt block. This is the point when you decide which T-shirt block will go where. As you know, based on your map, there are only so many choices that you can make. But within the constraints of your map, you will use color and the T-shirt content to decide where to place your T-shirts. You will also divide the T-shirts into sewing piles after their placement is determined.

Tools

- 48 count or larger box of coloring crayons
- Print-out or drawing of the quilt – the map
- The stack of cut T-shirt blocks
- Fat black Sharpie® pen

Step 1

The first step is to divide the design map into sections. Using a Sharpie®, divide the quilt into two to eight sections. The number of divisions depends on the size of the quilt. The larger the quilt, the more divisions you may have. Generally, each section will have between eight and 20 T-shirt blocks.

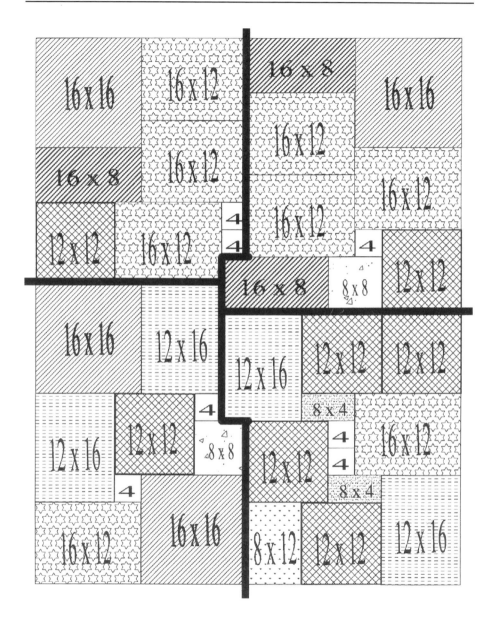

Use the natural break points to help you choose where to divide the quilt. Straight lines in the map are a good guide. Next, number each section. As you divide up the blocks, you will place them in the stack with the corresponding number to their section on the map. If you want, you can put a number on a piece of scrap paper for each section.

Step 2

I have found that spreading out on the floor gives me the space I need to sort out the blocks. On one side of me I have the stack of T-shirt blocks flipped over so they are upside down with the 16" x 16" blocks on top, face down. They still should be stacked from counting. If you are going to number your piles, spread the numbers out in front of you where each pile will be. Your color crayons should be on the opposite side of your stack of T-shirts. Also, set the map on something hard so you can write on it.

Step 3

Start at the top of your upside-down stack of blocks with the 16" x 16" T-shirt blocks. Begin by separating the colored T-shirt blocks from the gray and white T-shirt blocks. Next, starting with the colored blocks, decide where to place them one at a time. Color the

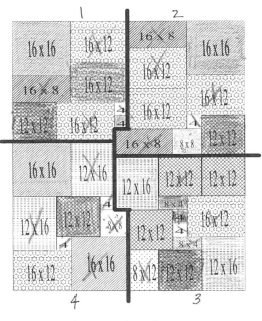

A completed map

corresponding block on the map with the color of the T-shirt block. If the T-shirt block is white, put an X on that block so you know there is a T-shirt block to go in that spot. If there are a lot of white T-shirt blocks of the same size in one section, you can write a word on the block from the T-shirt design to help you identify what T-shirt block goes in what spot. Then put the block in the pile with the corresponding section number.

Continue with the next block size until all the T-shirt blocks have been placed. If you have more T-shirt blocks than spots on your map or more spots on your map than T-shirt blocks, you may have miscounted. The blank 4" x 4" areas will still be unassigned. These blocks are added from the 4" x 4" blank blocks that you either cut now or when you are sewing. You can determine the color of these blocks based on the surrounding blocks or you can choose one color. Sometimes if I have cut a cool-looking tie-dyed T-shirt, I will use the leftover material from that T-shirt for all the blank 4" x 4" blocks.

Hints and Ideas

- Due to the binding, blocks placed on the outside of the quilt need to have more than a $\frac{1}{4}$" margin from the design to the edge of the block on the side touching the binding. Try to choose blocks with the design no closer than 1" from the edge of the block on the side that will touch the binding. Otherwise the binding may cut off the design on the T-shirt block.

- When considering placement of a block, study the design on the block. Designs where the subject is looking left or the action is moving to the left need to be on the right side of the quilt and vice versa for those looking right. Designs where the subject is looking up need to be in the bottom portion of the quilt and vice versa for those looking down. This is because the viewer's eyes tend to follow the action of the design.

- If there are two blocks from the same T-shirt of the same color (a front & back), try to place those T-shirts in opposite positions on the quilt. For example – one in the upper right quadrant of the quilt and one in the lower left quadrant.

- Consider assigning unique T-shirt blocks before the placement of the bulk of the blocks. For example, place a 8" x 16" hot pink block that has only one placement on the map before starting with the 16" x 16" blocks. This will help space out the other colored T-shirts more evenly.

- Big blocks should be assigned their location first because a big orange block has much more impact on the design than a small blue block.

- Try to distribute the colors evenly.

Double Check

You should now have a number of stacks of T-shirt blocks in front of you. Double check each section one at a time starting with section one. Work from one side of the section to the other, once again checking off each block on the map. Stack the blocks

T-shirt blocks split into four piles

Sections rolled up after having been check and stacked

on top of each other as they are checked off. When the section is complete and accurate, roll up the section – include the section numbers if you used them. Set the section aside (I use a plastic box) and continue checking the other sections until they are all complete. If one section is wrong, try to figure out what is wrong, and if necessary, go back and recount and redesign. If you have to do this, you will have to re-stack the T-shirt blocks.

Now that all of the sections have been checked and rolled-up, get out the sewing machine… it's time to sew!

Chapter 8

Sewing the Top

Sewing a T-shirt quilt top together is easy, fun and rewarding. It is surprising how fast the top will go together. An average size top can be pieced together in a morning. Compared to piecing a traditional quilt top, this is instant gratification!

Many misconceptions about sewing T-shirt material persist: the material is too stretchy, the material curls, and the material must be backed. The material is stretchy, but this is an asset, not a liability. Because of the stretch, it is easy to get even seams and matched corners. Yes, the material sometimes curls, but with practice and a few tricks, sewing T-shirt material may become easier than sewing the cotton traditionally used by quilters.

The misconception heard most about T-shirt material is that it must be backed with some type of backing or stabilizer such as interfacing. Working with T-shirt material is as simple as not mixing it with other types of non-stretchy fabric.

With an attitude that sewing this quilt top together will be easy, you will find that it is. But with any new skill, practice will make it easier. Before sewing the quilt top together, find the extra blank blocks you cut when you practiced cutting. These can be used to practice sewing blocks together. First, practice by sewing 4" x 4" blocks with the grain, then across the grain and finally with the grain mixed (one block with the grain going up and down and the other laid crosswise). Also, practice the start of the seam a number of times because that is the most difficult step. Also practice half seams which will be describe further on in the chapter.

Tools

- Sewing Machine with one of the following options:
  - Built in dual walking foot with ¼" quilting foot
  - Dual walking foot and ¼" seam market on throat plate
  - ¼" quilting foot
- White thread for bobbin and top thread
- Micro Sharp Quilting sewing machine needles #70
- Scissors - small

Sewing Set-Up

Set up your sewing machine with white thread in the top and bobbin. White thread works best because most T-shirts are white. Even when colored shirts are being sewn together, they most likely will be two different colors. And, most of the time, the stitches do not show through on the front of the quilt.

Use a very fine point needle. T-shirt material can easily snag or get holes in it. Finer needles reduce the chance of snags and holes. Also a finer needle makes it easier to start the seam. The stitch length should be 10 stitches per inch. This is the standard stitch length at which most sewing machines are set.

The best sewing foot choice is a built-in, dual walking foot with a ¼" quilting foot. A dual walking foot has top and bottom feed dogs that pull the top and bottom fabric through the machine at a uniform rate. Machines without a dual walking foot only have feed dogs on the bottom – so only the bottom fabric is being moved forward. The top fabric is just along for the ride.

Most machines do not have a built-in walking foot. There are some newer machines that, without the use of a dual walking foot, do a good job of moving both the top and bottom fabrics through the machine at a uniform rate. In this case, it would be better to use the ¼" quilting foot for sewing the quilt top. If your machine's feed timing is poor, then attaching a dual walking foot is advantageous. If you are using a dual walking foot that does not a have ¼" mark, mark the ¼" on the throat plate of your machine with either a Sharpie® or with masking tape. Practice both ways to see what works best for your machine.

One of the main tricks to sewing T-shirt material is to avoid having to pull out a seam. Removing a seam is very difficult. So, plan ahead before beginning any new seam. First, make sure that the seams are the same length and belong together. Second, check to see if the shirts are lined up in the correct direction and not upside down or backwards. And, last, double check what you are about to sew.

Part of your practicing should be removing a seam. After you remove a seam once or twice, it will be easier to remember to double check before sewing! The directions for removing a seam are on page 94.

> Note: All seams in the quilt top are ¼" seams.

Sewing

The first step is to line up the top of two blocks. Do not worry about lining up the entire seam, just the top corner and down about 3 inches. You will line the rest of the seam up after you have started sewing using the machine as a third hand. Next,

Lining up the corners

set the fabric under the presser foot and lower the presser foot down onto the fabric. The needle should enter the fabric on the first down stroke of the needle. The needle needs to enter the material about 1 mm in from the edge of the material. If the needle does not enter as such, the material runs the risk of being pulled down into the throat plate. Instructions on how to handle this situation are on page 92.

When the blocks are lined up under the presser foot, grasp the top and bobbin threads in one hand and position the threads to the back of the machine. When the machine starts, pull back on the thread. *This is a must!* If they are not pulled back when the machine is started, the fabric may be pulled down into the throat plate. Start the machine slowly while pulling back on the threads and pulling slightly forward on the material. This makes the machine take many tiny stitches which prevents having to back stitch at the start of the seam. Back stitching can also result in the fabric being pulled down into the throat plate.

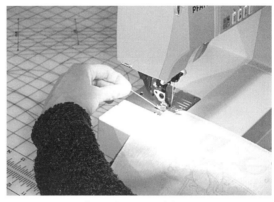

Starting position

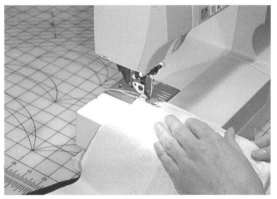

Continue sewing the seam

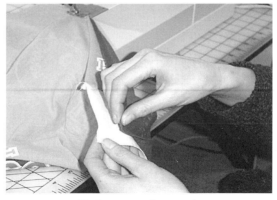

Lining up the ends

Lining up the rest of the seam

After you sew 8 to 10 stitches, release the tension on the fabric in front and continue to pull back until the fabric has advanced about an inch. Then stop and line up the rest of the seam. To do this, start from the bottom of the seam and match while moving up the seam. Just match the material in your hand pinching between your thumb and forefinger. Gather the material together as you work your way up the seam. If the seam is very long, start at the bottom and match the seams while moving up, pinning if necessary.

Remember, your quilt is built on a 4" grid. As you work, stop and measure the distance between blocks on the front

of the quilt to see if you lined everything up. The photograph to the left shows how your seams should not be. The intersection of blocks does not come together any where near perfect.

The photograph to the right shows the same seam with the blocks correctly lined up. To help determine how to line up your seams, use the 4" grid for a guide. You can fold a 16" wide block in half to find the 8" center. The 8" can then be folded in half to find the 4" mark. You can

pin the top together at the 4" intersections. The intersections might not always have an intersection of seams, but by using the grid you can line up the seam.

You will have to determine how perfect your seams will be. But if you look on the front and see an obvious error like the one illustrated on the previous page, you might consider taking the seam out and resewing it. To prevent having to remove a seam, you can pin at each 4" intersection.

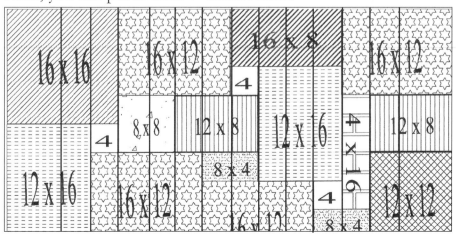

Escaping Tricky Situations

While you sew, some problems may arise that will require special handling. As you practice, many of these situations will become apparent. The following directions should help you work through and solve many of these problems.

Fabric Does Not Advance at the Beginning of a Seam

As discussed above, sometimes the fabric will get sucked down into the throat plate. This happens for a number of reasons: the needle was not far enough in from the edge of the material, the top and bottom threads were not held to the back while starting the machine, the wrong needle is being used, and best of all, no reason – it just happens. When this happens, **stop**! Do not try to continue, it only makes it worse. First, pull the blocks out of the machine by wiggling the hand crank wheel until the fabric is freed. Next, *do not pull out the stitches.* The stitches are really a knot. Pulling them out is very difficult and may put a hole in the seam. And since the knot is on the seam allowance, it should not get in the way. There are two options when this occurs. First, start the seam from the other end of the block. Or start over from the same end, but make sure to have the needle start in front of the knot. When starting again, pull not only the thread from the top and bobbin; also pull the threads from the knot.

One Block is a Little Longer Than the Other

This happens because some blocks are more stretchy than others. For short differences of a ½" or less, hold the ends together so they match and then pull gently together as you sew. For longer differences

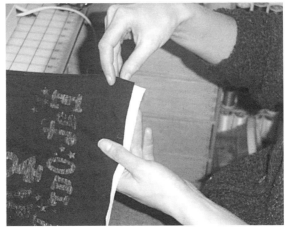

One block is longer than the other

greater than this, gently pull the short block and let the longer block flow through the machine unaided. Keep checking the length differences as you sew. When the difference in block lengths shortens to a ½" or less, switch to the technique for short differences.

The Fabric Rolls While Sewing

This will happen mainly on vertical seams because they are on the grain of the fabric. When this happens let the bottom block rest against the sewing machine and line up the top block over the bottom one by smoothing the top fabric down. When it is lined up, remove your fingers and sew a few inches. If the fabric was aligned before you started sewing, it should stay aligned. Although the fabric will curl back up when your finger is removed, the presser foot should flatten the material out as it is sewn. Repeat this process, working a few inches at a time until the seam is complete.

How to Rip Out a Seam

The trick here is not to get in a position to have to rip out a seam because it is difficult, it can put holes in the fabric and stretches out the blocks. So double-check the alignment and placement of the blocks before you begin sewing. To rip the stitches be sure that you only cut the stitches and not the material. You can work from the top of the seam or the inside. When you work from the top, use a stitch ripper to cut every third stitch and then lift off the thread on the back.

To work from the inside, gently pull the seam apart and clip the exposed stitch with either scissors or a dull small rotary cutter. Then gently pull the blocks apart to reveal more uncut stitches.

Chronological Steps to Sewing the Quilt Top Together

Choose a rolled section to work on. Find that section on the map and choose a starting place. The starting place should have the shortest seams and be a logical starting point. The concept to follow when building the quilt is to piece together small sections and then join them into larger sections. The larger sections are then joined to complete the quilt top.

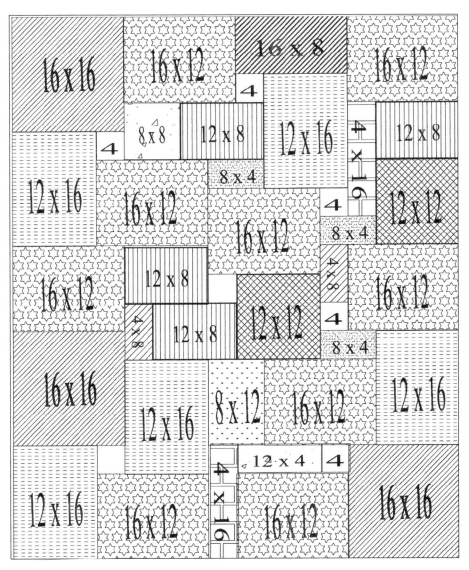

Full Top

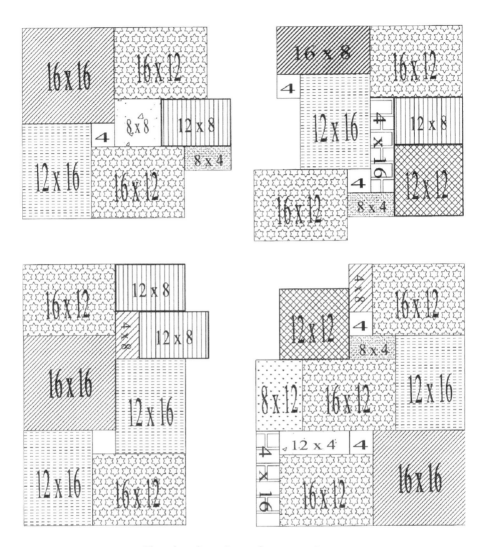

Top broken into four sections

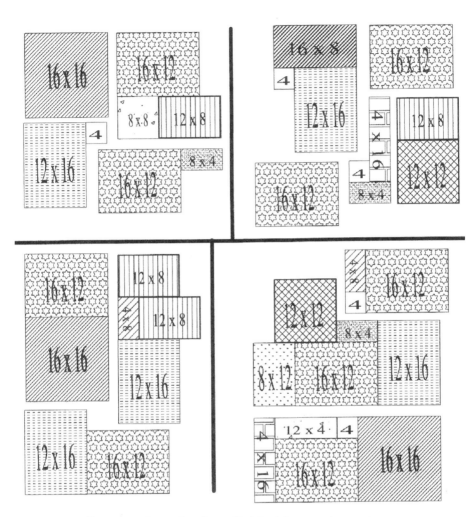

Four sections further divided into sub sections

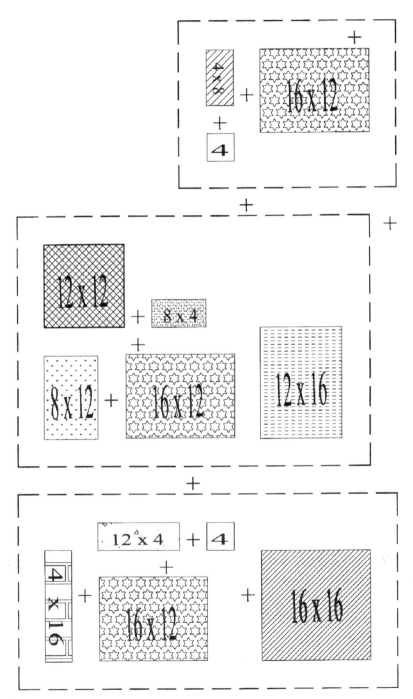

One section broken into three sewing sections

Half Seams

Not all the seams in the quilt can be sewn continuously because the blocks do not all intersect. When blocks do not intersect, you will need to use a half seam technique. First, two blocks are sewn together part way. Sew about half-way down the shorter of the two blocks and back stitch before removing the blocks from the sewing machine. The next block or section is then sewn to the first section along the section that had been made using the short seam. Continue building the section.

Eventually enough blocks are added to the section so the first half seam can be completed. Some half seams will not be completed until the entire quilt is nearly assembled. Many times, the last seam of the quilt is the joining of two half seams in the middle of the quilt.

Example of a half seam that is ready to be completed

Practicing Half Seams

If you have never used half seam construction before, here is a practice exercise. You need 5 blocks: 1 (4" x 4"), 2 (4" x 8") and 2 (8" x 4"). Lay out the pieces as follows:

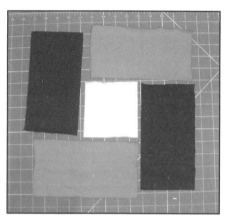

Lay out the five blocks as above. Remember that the 8" x 4" go across the top and bottom and the 4" x 8" are vertical.

The first seam is a half seam. Sew an 8" x 4" to the 4" x 4" - sew only about 2" and then stop.

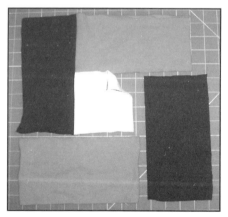

Next sew an 4" x 8" to the 8" section that was created by the half seam. Continue to work around the 4" x 4".

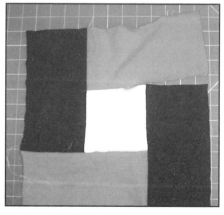

The last seam is the completion of the first seam.

Below is the sewing progression for the three sewing sections from the map on page 98. Each sewing section's progression is shown in a row. The progression continues on the next page with each of the sewing sections being pieced together into the quarter sub-section.

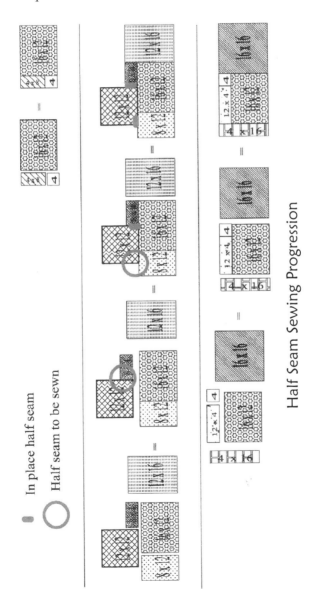

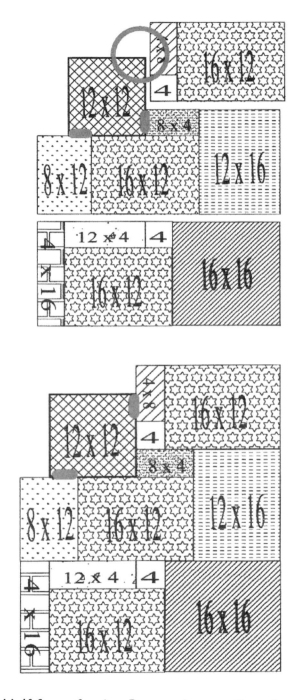

Half Seam Sewing Progression continued

Continue building sections until they are all completed. Then piece the sections together to make the top. When piecing the longer sections, be careful not to stretch the sections when moving them around. To join two sections, first check the map to determine what seam to sew first. Next, lay one section out on the floor or table. Take the opposing section and match it to the first section and then flip the second section over on top of the first. If necessary, pin at various points. Pinch together the starting points and gently gather the quilt along the seam line and set excess material on the table and in your lap. The long seams are sewn just as shorter seams are sewn.

Now that the top is together, spread it out on a bed and take a good look at it – this is about what the quilt will look like when it is completed. At this point, try not to handle the quilt too much because it will stretch due to the fabric and the weight of the quilt top.

A great part of this project is not having to iron any seams. So put your iron away. You are ready to move to the next step.

The next step is to prepare the quilt for quilting. This involves putting on a temporary binding. When the temporary binding is in place, the quilt is more stable and can be handled without fear of stretching.

Close up of TriDelt Sorority T-shirt Quilt

Chapter 9

Preparing to Quilt

In this section you will prepare your quilt to be long-arm sewing machine quilted, machine tacked, or hand tied. The first step is to sew on a temporary binding to keep the quilt from stretching out of shape. The second step is to prepare the material that goes on the back of your quilt.

Tools

For the Temporary Binding

- Rotary Cutter
- 3" wide x 30" long plastic ruler
- Rotary cutting mat
- Medium weight cotton - 2 yards
- Sewing machine
- Thread – any color
- ¼" quilting foot
- Scissors

For the Backing Fabric

- Fabric for the backing - types and amount described below
- Washing machine and dryer
- Sewing machine
- Thread to match backing fabric

Temporary Binding

A temporary binding is used to keep your quilt from stretching out of shape while it is being quilted. The binding is just a 1½" strip of material that is sewn around the four edges of the quilt with a narrow seam. After the strip is on, you can handle your quilt without fear of stretching it out of shape. This is a simple step, but it makes all the difference in the world in keeping your quilt square. *Do not skip this step.*

Choose a heavier weight cotton material for the strips. It needs to be heavier than quilting cotton but a blue jean material is too heavy. Look on the bargain racks for cheap material. *Do not wash the material* – the sizing helps keep the material stiff. And since it will get cut off and thrown away after the quilting is completed, it can be ugly.

Cut your strips from the long side of the fabric. Longer strips require less connecting seams which can save time. Cut the fabric on the grain. To set the fabric up to cut, fold the fabric so it falls straight from the fold. I have found that lining up the selvage edges may result in crooked strips. Then fold the fabric over again until it can be cut using a 30" ruler.

Begin by cutting a small slice off of one side to check for the accuracy of your fold. This test strip should be straight on the cut side and most likely it will be crooked on the selvage side. If you are happy with how your fabric is folded, begin cutting off 1½" strips. To have enough to sew on the four sides of your quilt, you will need to calculate the number of inches you need:

((Length + Width of quilt) x 2)+ 10 inches
Example: Quilt size 88" x 100"
((88" + 100") x 2) + 10"
= (188" x 2) + 10"
= 376" +10" = 386"

You may need to sew strips of temporary binding together to form a piece long enough for the side you are working on. You can either sew all the strips together at once or sew them together as needed. To sew the strips together use a simple straight seam. After you have cut your temporary binding and sewn the strips into long sections, you are ready to sew it on.

First, line up the upper right hand corner of the quilt face up with a strip of binding – good sides together. (See photo right). Using a ⅛" seam (half of the ¼" presser foot) sew from the top to the bottom of the right side of the quilt. It is very important

Temporary binding lined up on top of the quilt

that you do not let the quilt stretch at this time. So do not pull the quilt… let it feed naturally. To help keep the top from stretching as you sew the temporary binding on, fold the quilt accordion style and place the folds in your lap and the excess on the table.

Turing a corner

After the binding has been sewn to the right hand side of the quilt, fold open that temporary binding and then sew the bottom binding on. The second pieces of temporary binding starts at the top edge of the temporary binding from the prior edge. If you don't fold open the previous strip of temporary binding before sewing on the next piece of binding, you will have created a pocket and the quilt will not lay flat. Continue sewing on the temporary binding working around the quilt in a clockwise direction.

Note that you did not measure the length of the temporary binding, but rather you just sewed it on. I realize that for many of you this may not make any sense. The natural thought would be to cut strips of the same length for each side and to put the binding on the sides and then on the top and bottom. But through trial and error, I have found that this does not work. Because of the stretch of the fabric, the sides are not equal or don't sew equally. You will just have to trust me on this one. After the temporary binding is on you can handle your quilt top without the fear of stretching it out.

If you plan to have your quilt professionally long-arm machine quilted, you will need to mark the middle of the quilt on the top and the bottom temporary bindings. Begin by folding the top in half from side to side by grasping the two top corners of the temporary binding in one hand and grasp the middle with the other hand. Mark the center of the quilt on the temporary binding by either making a small cut ⅛" or less or by marking center with black marker. Repeat this for the bottom.

Backing Fabric

What fabric you choose to put on the back of your quilt depends upon the quilting method you choose. If you choose to long-arm machine quilt your quilt, use a solid color because it will show off the quilting. I have found that a 100% cotton or a cotton/polyester blend work well. If you are machine tacking or hand tying your quilt, you may want to choose a fun print that hides the ties or tacks. Any type of cotton or blend will work. Be sure that the material is not too heavy. If you are hand tying your quilt, be sure that a hand needle can easily be pulled through the fabric.

Whichever method you choose, make sure that the material you choose is machine washable. Also avoid stretchy materials – the top is stretchy enough. I have never used flannel because I do not like how it wears and it stretches too much.

Amount of Backing Material

The backing for most quilts will require two or three pieces of material to be seamed together to make one large piece of material. The directions here are for backings with horizontal seams.

To figure how much material you need for your quilt, add 12" to the width of your quilt and divide by 36" (1 yard). This equals the number of yards of fabric for one width.

Formula: (Width of quilt + 12") ÷ 36"
Example: Quilt size 88" x 100"
88" + 12" = 100"
100" ÷ 36" = 2.7 yards

Next, measure length of quilt, add 12" and divide by the width of backing material and round up to the next highest whole number. This is how many widths of fabric will be needed.

Formula:
(Length of quilt + 12") ÷ width of backing material
Example:
Quilt size 88" x 100"
Backing material = 45" wide
100" + 12" = 112"
112" ÷ 45" = 2.4 widths
Rounded up = 3

So the total amount of fabric you will need is the number of yards per width times the number of widths:

2.7 yards x 3 width = 8.1 yards

If you plan to bind the quilt with the same fabric that is on the back, additional fabric may be needed. So, in the example above, I would round my yardage up to 9 or 9½ yards. This should leave you enough backing material at the bottom or the sides of the quilt to use for the binding.

Washing

The first step in preparing the backing fabric is to wash and dry it. If the fabric will bleed, you will need to set the fabric's color with either a commercial product or with white vinegar. If you use a commercial product simply follow the manufacturer's directions.

To set your fabric with white vinegar, first wash your fabric in cold water with one Shout® Color Catcher. If the Color Catchers come out white or nearly white, your fabric does not need to be set and you can dry the fabric. If the Color Catcher

---

Hint: Cut a small ¼" triangle off each of the corners of the fabric before washing it. This will help cut down on the fraying of the fabric and helps keep the fabric from being twisted up in strings in the dryer.

comes out the color of your fabric, then you will need to set it with vinegar. Add 1 cup of vinegar in the washing machine with the fabric and soak in cold water overnight. Rinse and spin out the fabric in the morning or when you next remember it. Then launder as normal in cold water with 2 or 3 Shout® Color Catchers. If the Color Catchers come out white or nearly white, your fabric has been successfully set. If not, try washing it again with an additional few Color Catchers. If the second batch of Color Catchers come out white, the fabric color is set. If not, try to reset the fabric in white vinegar again. If you are unsuccessful after two attempts, start with a different piece of backing fabric.

After the fabric is set, dry it in the dryer and remove as soon as it is dry to help cut down on wrinkles.

Sewing the Seam

Unless you are using 108" wide fabric, you will have to

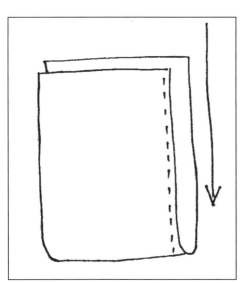

seam together your backing material. If you have one seam, begin by folding the material in half so the selvage edges are together and the right sides are together. (Left). Next, line up the top two corners on the same side of the material and sew one seam from the top to the bottom along the selvage edge. Doing it this way ensures that both pieces of material end up the same length. When you sew your seam, be sure to make your seam allowance wide enough that the selvage edge perforations and defects are inside the seam allowance. After you have sewn the seam, have someone hold the sewn end of the fold (or use a third hand device) and cut the fold open with scissors.

If you need to piece three lengths of fabric together, you will sew two seams. Begin by folding the fabric into three pieces. This is most easily done with another person's help. If you are unable to fold the fabric into three equal pieces, you can measure the length of the fabric and divide by three. Then measure out that amount and cut and then measure again and cut. Then sew the three pieces of fabric together. First, with right sides together, line up two corners. Then sew along the salvage edge from top to bottom. Next, line up the selvage side of the third piece of material to the selvage side of one of the previous pieces. Be sure that the right sides are together. Then sew along the selvage edges. Again, be sure your seam allowance is wide enough that the selvage edge perforations and defects are inside the seam allowance.

If you are going to have your quilt long-arm machine quilted, you will need to mark the center of the backing fabric on the top and the bottom in the same manner you marked the completed quilt top.

Your quilt is now ready to be put together. The next chapter describes how to quilt your quilt using a long-arm quilting machine, machine tacking, or hand tying.

Close up of my Dad's T-shirt Quilt
My Dad did not have very many T-shirts, but by adding colorful 4" x 4" blocks I was able to make him a cheery lap quilt.

Chapter 10
Quilting or Tying

Whether you decide to hand tie, machine tack or quilt your top with a long-arm quilting machine will depend upon what you have available to you and how soon you need the quilt. If you need the quilt now and are unable to get a spot with a machine quilter until three months from now, you may end up tying or tacking your quilt.

I have tried to quilt my quilts on a regular sewing machine a number of times and each time I didn't make it very far before quitting in frustration. Even with a hopping darning foot, the T-shirt material will be pulled and stretched. It just doesn't work.

Long-Arm Machine Quilting

If you are very lucky, you will have your own long-arm quilting machine. But if you are like most people, you will need to find a long-arm quilting machine quilter. If you need the name of a quilter in your area, check with your local fabric store, other quilters, your local quilt guild, or on-line.

After you find a quilter, you need to interview her to see if you like her work. First, ask to see samples of her work and check it for:

- Even stitches
- Smooth backing – free of puckers and folds
- Smooth front
- A square quilt that hangs straight.

Ask to see a quilt that is *not* "overall stitched" or "pantograph quilted" because your T-shirt quilt should not be overall quilted. Overall quilting is when the quilter follows a repeating pattern from the left to right across the quilt. Because of the stretch of the material, if an overall quilting pattern is used, the top will be pulled from one side to the other as the quilting is done. This in turn may not make your quilt square (more like a parallelogram). Another practice to avoid is computer-driven quilting patterns. The long arm machine operator needs to stand at the front of the quilt and use one hand to run the machine and the other hand to "work" the fabric. Occasionally, the material will need to be smoothed or manipulated. If the machine is driven by a computer and no one is watching, the T-shirt fabric may bunch or tuck. I think that T-shirt quilts look the best if each block is individually quilted. So you want a quilter who has experience and is comfortable with free form quilting.

You can also ask for references from other people for whom she did free form quilting. If she has not done free form quilting before, you need to think carefully about using this quilter. You may be able to get your quilt quilted at a reduced price while the quilter learns free from quilting. Or you may choose another quilter if you do not think that she is innovative or creative enough to do what you want. If all else fails, you can hire me to do your quilting. Visit my web site www.TooCoolTshirtQuilts. com - Make it Yourself - for more information.

Your quilter may have a selection of batting for you to choose from. I have been using a thin batting for years. Even with a thin batting, the quilt still is very heavy when it is finished. Most people are surprised at how heavy their quilt turns out. I use Hobbs Heirloom® Premium batting that is 80% cotton/20% polyester. I have never had any problem with shrinkage or washing over the years. And I have one quilt that has been washed 75 to 100 times and it still looks great.

A long-arm quilter should not shy away from this project for fear of the stretchy material. Because you put that temporary binding on your quilt, loading this quilt and quilting it on a long-arm machine should not be a problem. The quilter I used before I purchased my own long-arm quilting machine loved to do my quilts because it was a chance for her to be creative and to have fun. She was sad when I bought my own machine. See Appendix ii for samples of quilting designs for long-arm quilting machines that can be used on a T-shirt block.

Tying

Tying a quilt is the easiest way to hold your top, batting and backing together. It is done with simple knots that are tied about every 4 inches Note that the backing will be taped to the floor and the floor may get scratched from needles.

Tools

- Batting
- Fray Check™
- Long darning needles
- Masking tape
- Embroidery Floss – Color to match or contrast backing

- Backing
- Scissors
- Large clean hard floor
- Safety pins

Step-by-Step Instructions

Begin by cleaning your floor and preparing a work space that is large enough to lay out your entire quilt. Then tape down your backing material to the floor with the wrong side facing

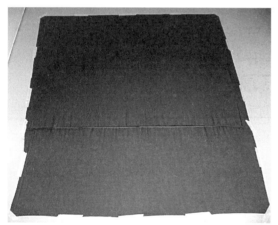

up. To ensure that the backing is flat and taut on the floor, tape in the following order: top center, bottom center, right center, left center, and then the corners. Last, fill in remaining areas between the centers and corners.

Backing taped to the floor

Next, lay out the batting on top of the backing. Follow the manufacturer's recommendation for how to use their batting. Be sure that the wrinkles are smoothed out before you lay the quilt top down. Lay the quilt top right side up on top of the batting smoothing out wrinkles as you work.

Batting on top of backing

The last step is to safety pin the backing, the batting and the top together. Pin the three layers together along the temporary binding about every 8 to 10 inches. Do not pick up the quilt yet. You will sew the ties while the quilt is taped to the floor.

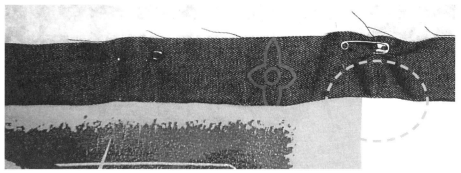

The backing, batting and quilt top safety pinned together in the temporary binding

The ties are made from 6 strand embroidery floss. Begin by cutting a piece of embroidery floss about 3 feet long and thread your needle. Make your first stitch 4 inches in from the side and the top. Take about a ⅛" stitch through all three layers. Hold back about 2" of thread before you start your first stitch. Sew in and out and then move 4" to the left or right to the next spot and

An untied stitch

take another stitch. Continue to move to the left or right (choose one direction to work) and continue sewing until you run out of thread. There should be at least two inches of thread at the end of your last stitch. Remember that the quilt is designed based on a 4" block. So determining where your stitches go should be easy if you just use the lines of the quilt to guide you.

Next, cut the embroidery floss halfway between the stitches. This should leave about 2" of thread on each side of the stitch. Next tie each stitch into a square knot. After all the knots have been tied, you need to cut the embroidery floss off on each knot to a set length. To do this, determine the length of embroidery floss you want hanging loose. Cut a piece of paper or an index card to the length you want and use it to measure all knots. Use this as a guge to cut the ties.

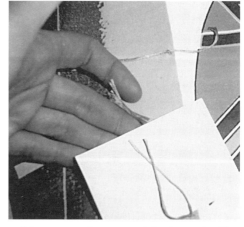
Use a card as a guide to cut all the knots off to the same length

Last, carefully remove the tape from the backing material and you can fold up your quilt. All you have left now is cutting off the temporary binding and sewing on the final binding.

> **Hint:** I have found a trick that will prevent the knots from coming untied in the future –
> Fray Check™! Simply put a drop of Fray Check™ on each knot and let the knots dry.

Machine Tacking

Another solution to holding the quilt top, the batting, and the backing together is to machine tack the quilt together with a standard home sewing machine. Your machine needs to have a button stitch.

Tools

- Batting
- Backing
- Safety pins
- Scissors
- Fray Check™
- Masking tape
- Large hard clean floor – the backing will be taped to floor
- Sewing Machine with a tacking stitch
- Feed dogs that can be dropped or covered
- Thread – color of choice – one or two spools

Step-by- Step Instruction

Begin by cleaning your floor and prepare a work space that is large enough to lay out your entire quilt. Then tape down your backing material to the floor with the wrong side facing up. To ensure that the backing is flat and taut on the floor, I tape in the following order: top center, bottom center, right center, left center, and then the corners. Last, I fill in remaining areas between the centers and corners.

Next, lay out the batting on top of the backing. Follow the manufacturer's recommendation for how to use their batting. Be sure that the wrinkles are smoothed out before you lay the top down. Lay the top right side up on top of the batting, smoothing out wrinkles as you work. The last step is to safety pin the backing, the batting, and the top together. Pin the three layers together along the temporary binding about every 8 to 10 inches. Then pin the entire quilt on the seams of the blocks every 8 to

10 inches. Be sure that you pin in the seams, you don't need any extra holes in the T-shirts. Last, remove the tape from the backing and pick up the quilt from the floor.

Safety pin in the seams
every 8 to 10 inches

Choose a thread color that either matches or contrasts with your backing. Wind at least two bobbins so you don't have to stop and re-wind while you are tacking. If possible, set your sewing machine up on the short side of a long table. This will give you room to rest the bulk of the quilt on the table. Next, set the machine to do a tack stitch about 2 mm to 3 mm wide. Then make a test sandwich of the backing, a piece of the batting, and a scrap of T-shirt material and test the stitch. You should stitch back and forth about 8 to 10 times on each tack.

When your machine is ready to go, roll the quilt in from both sides until just the center of the quilt is showing – about 10 inches wide. There are commercial clips that hold the rolls together that you may want to invest in. With the quilt laying in your lap, begin tacking at the top of the quilt and work down the quilt sewing machine tacking every 4 inches.

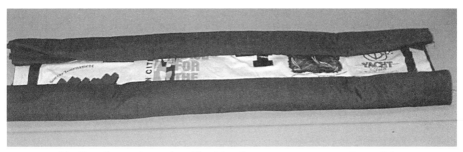

Quilt pinned and rolled in from two opposing sides

Between stitches, move the quilt down and do not cut the thread. As the quilt passes through the machine it will lay on the length of the table. I generally try to place the tacks in the seam allowance if there is one.

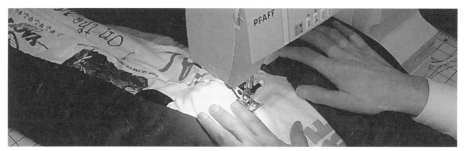

Machine tacking

When the last stitch is sewn in the bottom of the row, move the quilt over 4 inches and work back up the quilt. Remember that the quilt is designed based on a 4″ block. So determining where your stitches go should be easy if you use the lines of the quilt to guide you. Continue working from the center of the quilt out. You will need to re-roll the quilt every few rows.

When the entire top is tacked, before you cut the threads, place a drop of Fray Check™ on each tack on the front and back of the quilt. This will prevent the tacks from coming untied in the future. (Working in a well-ventilated room will keep you from getting a headache from the glue.) After all the tacks are in and glued, then cut the threads connecting the tacks. Since the tacks have been glued, you will not need to knot the threads.

You are almost done with your quilt. At this point, you have a good idea about how it will look. The next step is to cut off the temporary binding and get the quilt ready for its final binding.

Chapter 11

Cutting Off the Temporary Binding

Now that the quilting or tying is complete, the temporary binding can be cut off. The temporary binding, excess batting, and backing will be cut off with a rotary cutter in one cut. This creates a smooth edge on which to sew the final binding. At the same time you cut the binding off, you will be squaring the quilt up. Believe it or not, this is the messiest part of the whole process. When you are finished, small scraps will litter your floor.

Tools
- Rotary Cutter
- Large cutting mat – 30" x 36"
- 16½" square commercial Plexiglas® template with pre-printed grid lines
- 3" x 36" Plexiglas® ruler
- Table

The process of cutting off the temporary binding begins by squaring one corner, cutting that corner and then working around the quilt cutting the entire binding off. Begin by laying the quilt face up on a table on top of the cutting mat. The upper right hand corner of the quilt is on the mat. The rest of the quilt will hang off of the table onto the floor. Next, line-up your 16½"

16½" square template in upper right hand corner of the quilt

square template in the upper right hand corner of the quilt. If you are lucky, the template will square up with the block, but sometimes it does not line up. If this is the case, line up the template with the inside corners of the top block.

If worse comes to worse, eyeball it so the edges and block look square. The sides of your template should line up on the inside of the temporary binding.

Once the template is lined up, cut along the template on the two outside edges. Cut up from the bottom toward the top of the quilt on the right hand side of the quilt. Then move a quarter of the way around the table and cut along the top of

First cut

Second cut

the template. Cut through the excess material so that the corner of the temporary binding is cut off.

Next, move the quilt up from the bottom of the table, lifting and pulling up at the same time so the quilt does not get stuck on the cutting mat. Pull the quilt up far enough to leave about 6" of the already cut part at the top of the table. This will bring the right hand side of the quilt up to be cut. Then line up your 36" ruler along the inside of the temporary binding. The top of the ruler should line up with the already cut section. If the ruler is too far inside the temporary binding, you will have to move it slightly toward the binding ,trying to keep it as straight as possible. If the ruler is over the temporary

Top- First cut – right side

Middle - Approaching a corner

Bottom - Bottom corner

binding, gently pull the quilt from the binding side so the ruler falls on the inside of the binding. Cut along the ruler.

Continue to advance the quilt and cut along the side until you are about 15" from the next corner.

When you are about 15" from the next corner, line-up the square template in the corner and cut the corner as described above. Then turn the quilt 90° and continue cutting around the quilt until you are just about back to where you started.

Back around to the top side

When you get back to the top side and there is about 20" to 25" between the two cut sections, line up the ruler over the last uncut section using the two cut sections as a guide. If all went well, this cut should be straight. If not, you will need to eyeball it straight. Then make your final cut.

After I have cut the temporary binding off, I shake out all the little pieces from the quilt. Then I vacuum. You are nearing the end now. As you look at your quilt it will feel much more complete. The next step is to bind your quilt

Chapter 12

Binding and the Finishing Touches

The binding on a quilt is used to finish the edge of the quilt. The binding can also be used to add color to the quilt or tone down a bright quilt. If you have made other quilts, you can use the binding method of your choice. I use the method described below because I have found it to be durable and strong. It also matches the nature of the quilt.

Your choice of fabric for the binding can be any type of cotton or cotton/poly blend. The color can match or contrast with the backing. It can be a print in the same color family as the backing or it can be patched together from many colored fabrics. If your quilt is mostly white T-shirts, you may want to choose a brighter colored binding. For a quilt that has a lot of colored T-shirts, you may want to consider a more neutral color.

Tools
- Rotary Cutter
- Large Cutting Mat
- 3" x 30" ruler
- About 2 yards of cotton or cotton/poly blend fabric
- Fray Check™

Cutting the Binding Strips

The first step is to cut 3" wide binding strips from your fabric. Begin by folding the fabric in half so the selvage edges fall back on themselves and so you cut the length of the fabric. Fold the fabric so it falls straight from the fold. I have found that if you just line up selvage edges you may end up with crooked strips. Fold the fabric over again so it can be cut by a 30" ruler. Next,

cut off the selvage edge and check to see if your strip is straight and thus the fold is straight. Then cut your 3" strips.

Left: fabric falling straight from the fold.

Below: second fold

How Many Inches of Binding Are needed?

The formula for determining the number of inches of binding is:

Formula: ((Quilt length + quilt width) x 2) + 20 inches

Example: Quilt size 60" x 80"

(60" + 80" = 140") x 2 = 280") + 20" = 300"

So in this example, about 300" of binding will be needed. There are two ways to determine how many strips of fabric you will need to cut. The first is to divide the length of your strips into the total length needed and round up. Continuing from the above example:

Example: Fabric length = 72"

72÷300 = 4.16 → rounded up = 5 strips

After you have cut your strips, you may need to sew the shorter strips into longer strips.

How Sew Two Strips Together

If your binding is shorter than the side of the quilt you are sewing it onto, you will need to sew two or three strips of fabric into one long strip. Begin by laying one strip right side up with the end near you and the rest of the fabric laying to the left. Next, lay the corner of the next strip right side down on the first strip at a 90° angle. You will sew from the top left to the bottom right. You can do this by eye or your can draw a sewing line. Then sew the strips together. Cut excess material to leave ¼" seam allowance.

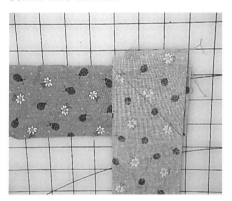

Two strips ready to sew

Sewing two strips together

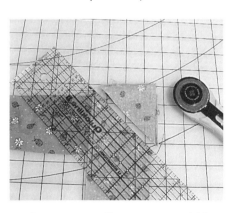

Trim seam allowance to ¼"

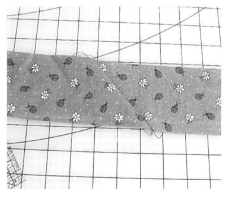

Binding folded open

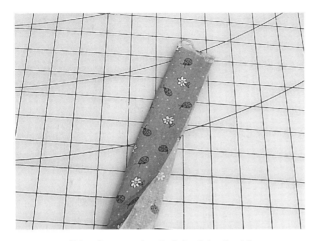

Binding strip folded in half

When you sew the strips onto the quilt, they will be folded in half lengthwise. You can either fold the strips as you sew or you can iron the fold in the strips before you sew.

Binding the Quilt

The right and left hand sides of the quilt are bound first and the top and bottom sides are bound last. So you will begin on the right hand side of the quilt. The binding takes two passes on each side.

First, fold the quilt face up in an accordion style so the folds lay in your lap and the bulk lays on the table to your left. Line up the top of your folded binding strip with the top right side of the quilt. The raw edge of the binding is lined up on top of the raw edge of the quilt and the folded edge of the binding is to the left. Your seam needs to be about ⅜" in from the edge of the binding and quilt. If

Binding lined up on quilt

you can line up your seam so the edge of the presser foot is on the edge of the quilt you will be able to sew a straighter line. You

 should try to sew as straight as possible so the finished binding is uniform. When you are lined up, sew from the top to the bottom of the quilt.

The second sewing pass is sewn from the front and catches the back of the biding on the back side of the quilt. First, refold the quilt to have the top right hand corner ready to sew, the folds in your lap and the bulk on the table to your left. Next, fold the binding around to the back of the quilt and down the edge of the quilt about 5". Sew on the front of the quilt about 2" down. Stay as close to the binding as possible without going on it.

As you continue sewing, fold the binding fabric around to the back of the quilt, pinching it in your left hand about 8" from the presser foot. Using your thumb and forefinger of your right hand, move the back of the binding back and forth to feel that the back of the binding is lined up. Do this down the 8" you are holding. You will feel the three layers of the quilt flatten out as you work your way down that section of the binding. Continue sewing down the quilt in this manner until you reach the bottom.

The stitches should be catching the binding on the back about 3/32" from the edge of the fold on the binding.

As you work, check the binding on the back to make sure the stitches are catching the back of the binding. If not, you will need to rip out the section where the binding was not caught and sew it again. After you fix the bad area, pull the threads from front to back, tie them off, and glue with Fray Check™. After you finish each side, check the entire length of the binding to make sure that the back of the binding was caught the entire way down.

After you sew the binding on the right side of the quilt, sew the binding on the left side of your quilt.

Top and Bottom Sides

Sew the binding on the top and bottom of the quilt the same as on the sides with the exception of the beginning and ending of the seam. I generally start on the bottom edge of the quilt and finish with the top edge of the quilt.

On your first pass on the bottom binding, instead of lining

Top - the binding is first extended two inches beyond the end of the quilt.

Bottom - the two inches are folded back over the back side of the quilt

The beginning of the first pass
on the bottom

Pull the binding up after
the first pass

the top edge of the binding with the top edge of the quilt, you will fold the binding back over the top edge of the quilt about 2". The 2" on the back should be caught in the stitching on the first pass. Then continue to sew the binding as you did on the left and right sides until you are about 5" from the bottom. At that time, cut the binding about 2" longer than the quilt and fold the binding around the bottom edge of the quilt. Again, the 2" on the back should be caught in the stitching on the first pass.

Before you begin your second pass down the binding, trim the seam over the 2" double back area off about ⅛". Next, pull the binding up where it is sewn over the top and bottom. Then fold the binding to the back to be caught in the final seam.

Now you are ready to start the final pass down the binding. Begin by folding the binding to the back for about 6" down the quilt. Check to see that the area at the start of the seam where the fabric is doubled over is laying flat and neat. When you start sewing the final pass, hold the quilt so the machine takes a number of small stitches to tack the seam. Normally, you would go forward and backward and then forward again to tack the beginning of the seam down. But I have found that if I do this, the back of my binding does not stay flat and neat. Continue working down the seam until you approach the end.

As you approach the end of the binding, you will continue to fold the binding around to the back. At the end you will also fold the doubled area over. At the very end of the binding, back stitch for about three stitches and forward for two more. I do not stitch off the end of the material; stop about a stitch from the edge.

Beginning at the end of the seam, pull the top thread through from the top to the bottom and tie a knot, cut, and glue

Example of the front and back side of the finished binding

with Fray Check™. Then move up the binding on the back to check that the binding was caught the whole length up. At the beginning of the seam, knot and glue the threads. Last, sew on the top binding as you did the bottom.

The Finishing Touches

Now that you have finished sewing you need to spend a little more time cleaning up your quilt. Working a quarter at a time, carefully check the front for any unclipped threads, clipping and gluing as needed. I also run a lint roller over the surface to clean up all the stings and fuzz. After I clean up the front of the quilt, I refold it into quarters with the back side up. I then clean up the back as I did the front.

The last step is the most important step – signing and dating the back of your quilt. Your quilt will be around for generations. Signing it helps future owners know its origins. I sign my quilts that have a light colored backing material with a permanent ink pen such as a black fine point Sharpie®. For the quilts with dark colored backing material, I use a silver permanent ink pen.

Now you are finished! Congratulations on making a Too Cool T-shirt Quilt!

Layout Counting Chart

Block Size	# of Block		Square Inches		Total Square Inches
16 x 16		x	256	=	
16 x 12		x	192	=	
12 x 16		x	192	=	
16 x8		x	128	=	
8 x 16		x	128	=	
16 x 4		x	64	=	
4 x 16		x	64	=	
12 x 12		x	144	=	
12 x 8		x	96	=	
8 x12		x	96	=	
12 x 4		x	48	=	
4 x 12		x	48	=	
8 x 8		x	64	=	
8 x 4		x	32	=	
4 x 8		x	32	=	
4 x 4		x	16	=	
Sum of total Square Inches =					
Square Root of Sum of Total =					

Sample Quilting Designs for Long Arm Quilting

Index